I0802454

GOD'S PRESCRIPTION FOR HEALING

Dr. Eriq and Lisa Harris

"He sent His Word and healed them ..."
Psalm 107:20

GOD'S PRESCRIPTION FOR HEALING

Scripture Therapy From a Cancer Survivor

APOSTLE DR. ERIQ T. HARRIS, SR.

Forewords by Dr. Donald L. Alford & Pastor Lisa Harris

GOD'S PRESCRIPTION FOR HEALING
Scripture Therapy From a Cancer Survivor

Printed in the USA

ISBN (print): 978-1-939944-41-2

ISBN (kindle): 978-1-939944-42-9

ISBN (epub): 978-1-939944-43-6

LCCN (Library of Congress Control Number): 2018941621

Cover Design & Interior Formatting: Wendy K. Walters

Published By

KINGDOM HOUSE
PUBLISHING

LAKEBAY, WASHINGTON

Scriptures have been taken from the King James Version of the Bible. The King James Bible is in the public domain.

To Contact the Author:

elderetharris@sbcglobal.net

FACEBOOK: Temple of Deliverance
Life Changing Ministries

https://www.facebook.com/TODLCM/?rf=196038543741501

"For I will restore health unto thee, and I will heal thee of thy wounds," saith the Lord ...

JEREMIAH 30:17a

Praise for God's Prescription for Healing

It is my joy to lend my voice with many others in celebrating Apostle Dr. Eriq T. Harris Sr.'s extraordinary testimony of victory over cancer. Truly, God will make a way where there seems to be no way. This Scripture-filled message of what God did for one person shows us that He can do this for anyone.

Dr. Harris has inspired the Body of Christ to go first to the kingdom of God and to seek healing through the declaration of His word, the Bible. As a cancer survivor myself, it is heartening to have validation of what God did in my life, and see what He has done for others. Apostle Eriq and Pastor Lisa have outlined the practical application of what to do when you are confronted with a diagnosis filled with fear and words that seem to say, "There is no hope." Truly, what you have in your hands is the right prescription: God and His word are critical parts of the remedy. I thank Dr. Harris for this inspired, faith-empowering book.

Trust in the Lord with all your heart and do not lean on your own understanding.
Proverbs 3:5

DANNY J. DEAN
An Apostle of our Lord Jesus Christ
Apostolic Director of Son Rise Cultural Center
www.sonriseculturalcenter.org
Navigator in the Courts of Heaven
www.courtsofheaven.org
Author of *Deeper Still* and *Poetry of the Dance*

Dedication

- To my mother and father, Albert and Hattie Stuckey, thank you for teaching me what unconditional love is; even when I was a child and made mistakes, you loved us in spite of them. Thank you for bringing us up in the fear of the Lord, bringing us to church and going yourself. Thank you for being my first love, Mom, and Dad, thank you for loving my mother the way you have. That's why I'm the man I am, the father I am, the husband I am, because of you.

- And, to my loving wife Lisa, Lisa, Lisa — it's hard to say your name just once because you mean so much to me. I can truly say that I never could have made it, never would have made it, without you. I would have lost it all but now I see, God brought you here for me. Thank you for saying "Yes" when I asked you to be my wife over 25 years ago. It seems like it was just yesterday and I'll never forget the day I first saw you. It brings tears to my eyes, just to think that God planned this holy marriage even before you were born. Babe, it would take a lifetime to tell you how much you really mean to me. Lisa, you will always be my wife, my friend, my lover, my personal prophetess, my girlfriend, my personal nurse; yes, Lisa babe, you are ALL THAT to me!

- I want to also dedicate this book to all my children: my oldest, Brittany Tyler Pye; my son–in–law, Daniel Pye; our wonderful new grandson, Dylan. Brittany, thank you for being my baby-girl, or as I would say when you were a little girl, my smurf. You made the devil to be a liar, when he said that you wouldn't be able to talk or hear or even function as a normal child. The Lord made all things work together for good! You finished grade school, high school, and college with above average grades, and I'm so proud of you! Now, thanks be unto God who always causes us to triumph in Christ Jesus.

- To my oldest son, Eriq Terrell Harris Jr., thank you for never giving up in life. Life was putting a lot of potholes in your way, but yet God has given you the grace to go around, over, and through them all. Son, you are an overcomer. I'm proud of you, son. The greater is coming for you, for when you seek first the kingdom of God, just because your route changed, your destiny remains the same, son. Remember God's word ..."*I know the thoughts that I have towards you, saith the Lord, thoughts that are good, not evil, to give unto you an expected end.*" Son, thank you for Ms. Rhi-Rhi, my first grandchild. Rhianna Marie Harris, you are a precious gift from God.

- To Emanuel Terrell Harris, my main man, my son, whom I love with all my heart—Manny, you are the apple of my eye like David was the apple of God's eye. I'm proud of you. The sky is the limit for the success in your life; just remember, if you delight yourself in the Lord, He will give you the desires of your heart. You are gifted, talented and smart, and your gifts will make room for you. You are also my Isaac, and I pray that the blessing on my life be released to you, as Jesus becomes Lord over your life!

- To Faith Monique Harris, my Angel, I believe that you were sent from God to teach me that all things are possible to those who believe. Faith, I'm so proud to say I'm your father. From the day you were born, you made me smile and I have been smiling ever since. You were born out of faith, being the first granddaughter born to the Harris family, so always remember if you put God first, you will never be last; you are the head and not the tail, above only, and not beneath. Faith, you are a gift not only to your dad, but to the body of Christ. Let the Lord continue to be the center of your life, and He will prosper you in all your ways.

- To Elijah Terrell Harris, EJ (or Ray) my youngest son, EJ, your dad sees so much in your future; it's so awesome, and it's going to be more than you can imagine. The hand of the Lord is all over your life, so you can do the will of God. I believe that the Joseph blessing is on your life, so no matter where you turn, the favor of God will be with you. All of your life you will have favor with God and man. This favor is passed on from your dad and grandfather, Rev. Mosezel Fleming, who have touched many people's lives, and that anointing is on you to change a generation to come with your life and the word of God. Keep this in mind: (EJ) seek ye first the kingdom of God and all things will be added unto you! You are going to be blessed and a blessing. When I look at you, son, I see your granddad (paw-paw) smiling through you. I'm proud of you son.

- To my six brothers and their families:

    - To my twin brother Pastor Derik Harris, my best friend; and to Shirley Harris, Kendrick Harris, Kaden Harris, Christian Harris, Major Harris, Brandon Harris, Monica Harris, Rashetta Harris.

    - To Tony Harris Sr. and Tony Harris Jr.

    - To Carlos Harris Sr. and Tamia Harris, Carlos Harris Jr., Teyton Harris, Trinity Harris, Trenton Harris, Trinece Harris. To Allen Harris Sr. and Allen Harris Jr., Amir Harris, Amber Harris. To Gregory Harris, Derrick Harris.

    - To all of my brothers and their families, thank you for your love and support.

- To my special God-daughter (Ms. Cee) Cierra Turner and Denise (pumpkin).
- To one of the best sister-in-laws in the world, Sharon (Wardell) Durrett (Tiffany).
- To the greatest mother-in-law, EVER—Eldora Fleming, thank you momma for your love and support to Lisa and our beautiful children. You are always mentioned to God in my prayers. I speak life, love and peace over you forever.
- To my favorite aunt, Rosie Burgess and family, and the Moore family.
- To my favorite cousin, Florida Williams and family.
- To my uncle, Melvin Ivy.
- To Uncle Joey and Pearl Blakey (Indianapolis, Ind.), thank you for loving me when I lost my father (John Eddie Smith) as a child. I will never let God forget what you two did for us.

Special Thanks

I would like to give special thanks to some people who have gone on before me, but have played an important role in my life:

Late Albert Stuckey Jr. (Dad - Stuckey)

Late Rev. Mosezel Fleming (Father-in law: Paw-paw)

Late Augusta Mason (Grandma Gussie)

Late Lizzie McDonald (Anne)

Late Archie Mason (Great-Grandfather)

Late Bishop Gilbert E. Patterson (Great-Great-Uncle)

Acknowledgments

To my best friends:

Pastor W. Charles Morrow

Dr. Steven L. Pettis Jr.

Pastor Danny Norment

Elder Tondalah and Walter Stroud (F.O.G.) Cosmetic

With gratitude to:

Apostle Dr. Sylvester P. Brinson III

Apostle Dr. Bruce Cook

With special love for:

Temple of Deliverance Life Changing Ministry Family

Dr. Betty Johnson and family

Elder Debra Cody and family

Minister Eric and Letrice Winslow family

Elder C. Gaines and family

Sis. Cynthia Washington and family

Bro. and Sis. Oyungo and family

Evangelist Bell and family

Bro. and Sis. Nichole Smith-Wilson

Evangelist Nick and Rene Powell

Min. McKay and Evangelist McKay

Evangelist Nichole Jackson family

Mother Samuel and family

Mother Houston and family

Mother Harris and family

Longstreet and Armstead families

Sis. Erica and Trina Winslow and family

Derrick Orr, Former Principal, Manierre Elementary School

Dr. Tinishi Davis, Principal, Manierre Elementary School

With distinctive acknowledgment to:

Apostle Donald L. Alford and Pastor Gloria Alford & Progressive Life-Giving Word Cathedral family.

To our spiritual parents: It means so much to us that God brought you both into our lives. From the day you became our spiritual covering, we knew what we were called to do. The Word of God is true, and the Words that you spoke unto us were Spirit and they were Life. Thank you both for being role models to us; we will always treasure the love, teaching and support that you have given us.

CONTENTS

xv Foreword by Dr. Donald Alford

xvii Foreword by Pastor Lisa Harris

xxvii Introduction

1 Chapter 1
HE SENT HIS WORD AND HEALED THEM

7 Chapter 2
GOD GAVE ME A YES!

15 Chapter 3
DON'T TELL ME IT'S TOO LATE

21 Chapter 4
GOD'S BENEFIT PACKAGE

27 Chapter 5
HEALING IS A GIFT FROM GOD

35 Chapter 6
GOD CANNOT LIE

43 Chapter 7
HOW TO RECEIVE YOUR HEALING

49 Chapter 8
KEYS TO UNLOCK YOUR HEALING

55 Chapter 9
TESTIMONIES AS A RESULT OF THE HEALING

67 Chapter 10
HEALING SCRIPTURES AND CONFESSIONS

85 Meet the Author
DR. ERIQ T. HARRIS, SR.

Foreword by Dr. Donald Alford

This book, *God's Prescription for Healing*, written by my spiritual son, Apostle Eriq Harris, will encourage anyone who has been or is currently in a faith battle. His story of healing and the entire process of his victory will inspire and provoke individuals to consider going to the next level of faith for their personal health challenges. I am so godly proud of Apostle Eriq & Pastor Lisa Harris, who continue to impact the Kingdom for God's glory. This is a must read book. We look forward to hearing all of the wonderful testimonies that will materialize as a result of reading this literary and spiritual masterpiece by Apostle Eriq Harris. Thank you Son for supporting your spiritual Dad for over 20 years!

DR. DONALD L. ALFORD
Apostle and Bishop
Progressive Life-Giving Word Cathedral | Hillside, Ill.
www.plgwc.org

"This sickness is not unto death."

JOHN 11:4

Foreword by Pastor Lisa Harris

"So they are no longer two, but one flesh. Therefore what God has joined together, let no one separate."

MATTHEW 19:6, NIV

I married Eriq Harris on August 15, 1992. I spoke vows at our ceremony and took to heart those words *"for better or for worse, in sickness and in health."* Married life was blessed; I finished nursing school and began working. We worked, loved the Lord, enjoyed our family of five and loved the ministry of being a servant as Pastor and First Lady.

One evening July 2, 2007 while at gymnastics class with our youngest daughter, Faith, I received a phone call from my husband. Eriq was not feeling well, and was experiencing unbearable abdominal pain. He told me that his twin brother, Derik, was going to take him to the Emergency Room and for me to meet him there. I knew at that point something must not be right; Eriq said he doesn't go to the doctor. A few days earlier, he had experienced an upset stomach. We took no thought of the matter. I thought to myself, 'You are so far north, you cannot possibly get home that quick and it's rush hour.' I began to pray. I knew and reminded myself, that God is omnipresent.

Medication was given and Eriq was sent home. The doctor had given us an appointment date to see his primary doctor 18 days later. Five days after that, a colonoscopy was scheduled to take an in depth look into the stomach. On the day of testing, something just did not feel right within my spirit. I continued to pray and after several hours, a nurse came and told me the doctor would like to see me for a moment. While waiting in this small office, I heard the Lord say, "This sickness is not unto death..."

The doctor then came into the room and said to me, "The results do not look good." I turned to him and said, "What stage is it?" The doctor looked at me strangely and asked, "Did my fellow doctor just leave from here talking to you?" "No," I replied. For I knew it was my doctor, the Holy Spirit, who was just talking to me and preparing me. A biopsy was shortly performed, and Eriq was returned back to his room.

The doctor said to both of us, "As I was telling your wife, we saw a large mass and did a biopsy of your tissue. We will get back with the two of you as soon as we get the results." We embraced each other and left the consultation room. That was the longest walk ever to the parking lot, but I kept a conversation going with Eriq to keep his mind clear. We sat in the car, had prayer together and drove home.

On the ride home, I could hear the Holy Spirit say again, "My daughter, this sickness is not unto death, but for the glory of God that the Son of God might be glorified thereby" (John 11:4, KJV). So, with replaying the Scripture which the Holy Spirit had just spoken, and hearing the doctor say, "We will do further testing," but never answering me when I asked what stage, my mind could only hear cancer, but I dared not say it to myself or my husband. That evening we had dinner with family, watched a movie together, had prayer and went to bed.

Can you imagine being awakened July 26, 2007 with a call from the doctor, on the third day after the testing, to get the news that you have Stage 3 cancer?! Well, that's the call my husband received. I sat up in bed as my husband looked astonished on the phone and then he fell to his knees from the side of the bed, saying, "NO!" In that moment, I then looked into my husband's eyes and said, "We will get through this." Of course, I had a moment of pity, since this now was a fact that Eriq had been diagnosed with cancer, but truth is stronger than facts, and the truth of the matter was, my God is a healer. I quickly got up and said, "This battle is the Lord's." God said that by His stripes we are already healed.

I could not imagine what was going through Eriq's mind. I could only pray for peace and continue to love on him while quoting the Scripture, *"For God has not given me the spirit of fear but of peace, love and a sound mind."* I then said to myself, 'You have to be strong for Eriq and the family.' Part of my marriage vow was "in sickness and in good health." I was so angry with the enemy that I told him (satan) this weapon (cancer) will not prosper. God's word says, *"No weapon formed against you shall prosper..."* (Isa. 54:17). I was also reminded that Eph. 4:29 says, *"Let no corrupt communication proceed out of your mouth, but that which is good to the use of edifying, that it may minister grace unto the hearers."*

I spoke life into my husband every day and night in spite of the doctors' reports – no matter what his test results revealed, and no matter what his physical appearance was being changed into. When I would receive a phone call from family and friends, I would find myself encouraging them.

I now had to change my thinking. I was determined not to let any negative thought, behavior or any negative influences from the outside come near my dwelling. I begin to clean the house even more, to keep my mind occupied. For, I was reminded of the Bible story about Jairus' daughter. On the way to their home, Jesus stopped to heal a woman. Upon arriving at Jairus' house, people replied to Jairus, "It's too late; she is dead." Jesus heard what was said and immediately replied to be not afraid, but believe. However, many people were crying over the death of the little girl Tabitha. Jesus then said she is not dead but sleeping.

When family and friends heard about my husband's condition, they, too, began to talk. No, he was not dying, but their negative talking and response was death. I even had a parent from school stop me to say, "Oh, I saw your husband and he doesn't look good. He has lost so much weight; you know, my grandmother died from cancer." I immediately said, "It is not so; death shall not come near him. This sickness is not unto death, so if you cannot stand here and encourage me, then I would rather you keep silent." We parted our ways.

I even had some comment, "You are going through a lot. Your oldest daughter has gone away to New York for college, your youngest daughter is accepted into a gifted school on the north side, then you have the boys. How are you going to do all that and the church?" I simply replied, "I can't, but I can do all things through Christ Jesus who strengthens me, according to Philippians 4:13." So, back to the Bible story, as Jesus saw the fear of the people, he had everyone leave the home of the girl except his disciples, Jairus, and his wife. When negative talk came around Eriq, I immediately shut it out. I did not want his ear gates to hear anything or anyone that was not speaking life.

My home was constantly saturated with worship music. I began to screen all phone calls. I would not even allow people to bring over food that they had cooked. It's not that I didn't appreciate their cooking. However, cancer cells thrive on certain ingredients and food. I began to pray and ask God what to do.

"Howbeit that was not first which is spiritual, but that which is natural; and afterward that which is spiritual."

1 CORINTHIANS 15:46

The natural body is flesh and blood, consisting of bones, muscles, nerves, veins, arteries and fluids; and, as such, it is of a corruptible frame and form. The natural body is liable to break down, decay and deteriorate.

I began to do research on the various types of food that cancer feeds on. Every food that contributes to the vitality of cancer, I began to filter from my kitchen. Those foods were no longer on my grocery list. I even searched for and found an alternative nutrition center in Evanston, Ill. We were able to target foods that would inhibit and not promote the growth of cancer, nor weaken Eriq's cells. As the chorus of a familiar hymn says, "What can wash away your sins, nothing but the blood of Jesus, what can make you whole again, nothing but the blood of Jesus!"

In an adult of average size, there is a little less than 10 pints of blood, according to *Rush-Presbyterian-St. Luke's Medical Center Medical Encyclopedia Wolrd Book, 7th Edition.* Chicago: World Book, Inc. 1995. Blood is the fluid that transports nutrients and oxygen to the cells in your body. It also takes away wastes from your body and fights infection and carries chemicals that regulate many body functions.

Not only did I apply natural change but spiritual; I applied the word. I spoke healing Scriptures and interceded for my husband. I prayed with and for my children. The children even prayed for their dad. I supported my husband and allowed him to participate in the activities with the children as much as he could. I reminded God of His word that by His stripes we are healed (Isa. 53:1). The Bible says according to 3 John 1:2, *"Beloved, I wish above all things that thou mayest prosper and be in health, even as thy soul prospers."*

> Not only did I apply natural change, but also spiritual

After we received the confirmed results of his Stage 3 cancer diagnosis, everything began to move so quickly. Three days after the notice, I had to leave and go speak at a women's conference. My children had dentist and doctor's appointments, followed by going to the new elementary school for registration and completing college freshman orientation forms. Eriq had to have various testing and lab work done in order to prepare for chemo and radiation treatments. He was determined for this not to interrupt our daily lives. We drove our daughter 12 hours to New York, where she was about to start the next phase of her life as a college student. Since she was many miles away from home, we decided not to tell her the news until she came home for Thanksgiving.

August 20, 2007 Eriq had outpatient surgery for insertion of a port-a–cath. The port-a-cath is a proprietary, indwelling device that provides long-term IV access for administering TPN, blood products, drugs, and high-dose chemotherapy. Daily chemo and weekly radiation treatment began on August 27, 2007. Eriq was exhausted, and I was exhausted; yet, whenever he would turn to me, God gave me enough strength to smile back at him and say, "We can do it." Now, hear me; although he was the one going through daily treatments and chemotherapy, I felt every pain and groan he experienced.

God is so awesome; in the midst of everything that was going on, He kept my mind strong. Isa. 26:3 says it best this way: *"Thou will keep him in perfect peace, whose mind is stayed on thee: because he trusteth in thee."* I thank God for my sister and mother; they helped out tremendously with the kids as well as my mother in law. I was blessed to have church members and families who would come get the kids and take them out so that they could maintain their daily activities.

Daily chemo and weekly radiation would leave Eriq exhausted and very weak. His nutrition became unbalanced, as he was fluctuating between having a desire to eat, and being unable to eat, along with needing to eat, but no desire to eat and weight dropping uncontrollably. There were many times we would go to see the doctors, and they would constantly say, "Eriq, you have to eat something." They even suggested in no uncertain terms that he go out and eat a burger or steak. "You need to eat!" I began to pray that his taste buds would line up and function in the perfection that God had created them to function.

There were times that the senior doctor would say, "You are at this stage and yet you are not experiencing the usual symptoms: sores in your mouth and even depression and even uncontrollable anxiety at this stage. You are one of the very few patients I've seen that does not show the normal side effects from such a hard hit of chemo and radiation." The senior doctor thought that it was strange the symptoms were not occurring and would say, "I know, I know; it's the man upstairs, right?" My response was, "To God be the Glory!"

Just to mention a few side effects of treatments, Eriq did experience the burning and peeling of his hands and feet. In the natural, I would apply a mixture of Aquaphor® healing ointment with virgin olive oil and in the Spirit, apply the word of God. When Eriq experienced loss of appetite, I would make healthy smoothies that were infused with vitamins and minerals that would lessen the symptoms he was experiencing. I would cook the foods that were his favorite using different herbs and pray as I stirred. I spoke to his internal organs before and during meals as he ate.

Once a week, we had to go for infusion treatments. During this time, while sitting in the waiting room to be called on or even while sitting in the infusion room, the Lord would send someone, even non–Christians, for us to minister to. According to Rom. 15:1, *"We then that are strong, ought to bear the infirmities of the weak, and not to please ourselves."* So, even in my weakness as well as my husband's weakness, His strength was made perfect.

Throughout treatments, surgeries and physical changes in my husband's body, I never lost hope. I kept the faith. When his weight would drop dramatically, I would either buy new garments or take his favorite clothes to receive alterations. At times when the enemy would try to come in and let me see my husband in his natural state, I would say, "Lord, I look unto the hills from whence comes my help; it all comes from you, Lord. Now, Lord, do what only you can do. Let me see my husband as you see him."

Early one morning, on Nov. 17, 2007, I was awakened by the sound of Eriq moaning. I saw him sitting on the side of the bed as I begin to call his name, but he would not answer. I could see him sitting there gazing stone-faced into the air. I began to shout his name. Not responding, he slowly began to slump over onto the bed. I became very anxious and a spirit of anxiety overshadowed me and I heard the enemy say, "Look at you now; you will be a widow soon." I immediately begin to plead the blood of Jesus, calling out frantically to awaken my oldest son and his brothers. As I dialed 911, I continued to plead the blood of Jesus as the paramedics arrived and tried to get Eriq to respond. He was admitted into the local Emergency Room and once again, God showed up and healing took place.

I had to be strong not only for my husband and self, but also for the children and family. God began to give me such an insurmountable strength that I knew was not of my own. I continued to pray, fast, anoint my husband's body and intercede for him. God gave me grace to be there for my husband and family as well as for the church.

According to Isa. 55:8, *"For my thoughts are not your thoughts, neither are my ways are not your ways, saith the Lord."* Several weeks prior to Apostle Eriq's sickness, the church was in transition. The leasing property was taking a toll on the finances of the church, and at the same time, we were asked to help build and encourage another church.

God had it all planned out, though; we were in a place that while Eriq was going through his life and death health challenge, our congregation would still be together in one place and in one accord. While our church helped minister to another church in their time of need, God met our needs. I did not have time to worry for the Bible says, *"Take therefore no thought for the morrow: for the morrow shall take thought for the things of itself. Sufficient unto the day is the evil thereof"* (Matt. 6:34).

I give all the glory and honor to God for manifesting His healing power. I say to you: stand still and see the salvation of the Lord. I reminded the Lord according to Isa. 55:11 that He said, *"So shall my word be that goeth forth out of my mouth: it shall not return unto me void, but it shall accomplish that which I please, and it shall prosper in the thing whereto I sent it."* The Lord sent His word and healed him. Hallelujah. For without faith it is impossible to please the Lord. You can't watch, harbor or give in to fear and think it will produce faith.

Be encouraged, you who may be reading this now and are going through a fiery trial or test with a loved one who was given a report of cancer or any sickness. The Bible confirms in Jas. 5:14-15, *"Is anyone among you sick? Let him call for the elders of the church, and let them pray over him, anointing him with oil in the name of the Lord and the prayer of faith will save the sick, and the Lord will raise him up. And if he has committed sins, he will be forgiven."* Ask the person with the sickness to confess their sins, and in your daily prayer time, include the following:

- Worship music
- Healing Scriptures
- Decree and declare that the assignment of sickness is canceled.
- Speak and command the sickness to leave.
- Declare the symptom you see to leave.
- Command every part of the body to line up with the word of God and declare that the body parts function in the perfection God created them to function.

- Command that the cancer cells will not multiply.
- Command that the radiation will not affect the good (healthy) cells.
- Curse the cancer cells to be destroyed and leave the body, and command that they do not come near the healthy cells as they exit.
- Command that the body will not reject the chemotherapy.
- During the feeling of loved one being nauseous from medical treatment, command the stomach to hold down the food intake.
- Declare that the spirit of fear does not come near your loved ones' presence.
- Command every negative person's mouth to be shut.
- Declare that the will of God be done on earth as it is in heaven.
- Call on Jehovah–Shalom; don't ask God to give peace, for He is peace. Call Him and He will answer (Jer. 33:3).

I've seen Him do it! Hallelujah!

I speak forth comfort at this time and I pray that the Almighty God rest upon your heart, in Jesus name. Amen.

LISA HARRIS
Pastor
Temple of Deliverance Life Changing Ministries | Chicago, Ill.
www.facebook.com/TODLCM

Introduction

"He sent His word to heal them from their destructions."

PSALM 107:20

It was prior to the year 2007—maybe about three years off and on—and I was having pain in my abdomen. I thought maybe I should watch what I eat, and also what I allow to stress me out. I didn't have any idea what was going on. Then, I began to notice blood in my stool; at that point, I said to myself, "Maybe I'm straining too much. I should be careful lifting large items." Just like most men, I was trying to do anything but admit I should see a doctor about this. Finally, I shared this with my wife Lisa, and she insisted that we see a doctor right away, but I kept putting it off. "I'll go next week," was my standard response. The pain would go away sometimes for weeks, but then come back. When it came back, so did the blood in the stool, so my wife thought this might be a bleeding ulcer.

By July 2007, the pain was unbearable, so we went to the Emergency Room (E.R.) at a local hospital for treatment. After the E.R. visit, we followed up with my doctor, to schedule my first colonoscopy on July 24th in the GastroIntestinal Department. I remember July 26th so well, like it was yesterday. The doctor called and said to me, "Mr. Harris, you have Stage 3 colon cancer."

It seemed as though everything was going in slow motion. I fell to my knees and said, "No! No!" Lisa asked me, "Babe, what's wrong?" I told her and she put her arms around me and said, "We are going to fight this and we are going to win."

We began to pray together, and, after praying, I felt the Lord's strength come upon me. His strength became perfect in my weakness. I began to hear my Apostle Donald L. Alford say, *"The words that I speak unto you, they are spirit and they are life."* I knew that being diagnosed with Stage 3 cancer, I would need God's life-giving word to fight for me.

Due to being in Stage 3, I needed aggressive treatment, along with surgery, daily radiation and chemotherapy, which lasted for months. I remember having to have a port put in my chest, so that the chemo could be administered, and a colostomy bag was next, which was hard for me to understand how would I be able to stool in a plastic bag taped and hanging from my stomach. At that point I needed God to keep my mind stong, because I couldn't understand that at all.

At that time the enemy (satan) tried to attack my mind, as I was on the table daily for radiation. He (satan) said that I wasn't going to live, but I knew what God's word said, "Life and death are in the power of my tongue," so I never repeated what satan said, no matter how I felt, or how much weight I lost, and I lost a lot. I never even said I had cancer throughout the whole process, while my weight dropped from 210 lbs. to 150 lbs.

The Bible says that all sickness is not unto death, so I began to speak life over myself, and continue to say, 'I shall not die but live.' The Scripture that was a great comfort to me was Rom. 8:32, *"He that spared not his own Son, but delivered him up for us all, how shall he not with him also freely give us all things?"* Since God freely gave me His son, then why wouldn't He freely give me healing? Since I have Jesus on the inside, then greater is He in me, than the cancer.

People would ask me, "Was it hard battling cancer?" I said, "No, I wasn't battling cancer; this fight was between God's word and cancer." Heaven and earth shall pass away, but the word of our God SHALL stand firm forever.

Heaven and earth shall pass away, but the word of our God SHALL stand firm forever

On December 3rd, 2007 the colostomy bag was removed, and on December 21st, 2007 the chest port was removed. On January 16th, 2008, the surgery to close the Ileostomy stoma in my stomach was performed and it was closed.

I returned home cancer free! To God is the GLORY for the things He has done. I continued to follow up with my radiation, chemo, and surgical doctors on a regular basis until 2010; after that, it was once every other year. September 18, 2013—two days after my 48th birthday—I went in for a colonoscopy, and satan tried to talk to me and bring fear that when you go back in this time, it will come back (cancer). The word of God reminded me in Nah. 1:9 "*… whatever they plot against the Lord, He will make an utter end; affliction shall not rise up a second time!*" Amen.

Yes, I took my treatments, and medication as prescribed, but I also took God at His word. His word is medicine for my mind, body, and soul. It was eight years later in 2016 when I began to write this book, letting you know that God has no respect of persons if you trust Him. God is the same yesterday, today and forevermore.

Apply God's word to your everyday life; if you work the word, the word will work! One of my favorite Scriptures comes from Hab. 3:19, which says, *"The Lord is my Strength, and He will make my feet like hinds feet, and He will make me to walk upon mine high places."*

Read and meditate on the promises of God that I'm sowing into your life through this book and live! God bless you!

The word of God is medicine for the mind, body, and soul. 3 John 1:2 says, *"Beloved, I wish above all things that thou mayest prosper and be in health even as thy soul prospereth."* Take ALL of what THE Great Physician (God) has prescribed for you in His word. When a human medical doctor prescribes medication for a patient, it's to be taken until all the dosage is finished.

Matt. 5:18 says, *"For verily I say unto you, till heaven and earth pass, one jot or one tittle shall in no wise pass from the laws till (all) be fulfilled."* So, I prescribe to you to read over the word of God two to three times a day, if you are in need of healing. Allow the Holy Spirit to build your faith as you read these words of life.

John 6:63 says, *"It is the spirit that quickeneth; the flesh profited nothing: the words I speak unto you, they are spirit and they are life."* Speak the words of life over yourself in the first person tense, laying claim to them by faith, with the understanding that they are your inheritance as a child of God.

1

HE SENT HIS WORD AND HEALED THEM

"He sent His word, and healed them, and delivered (them) from their destructions."

PSALM 107:20

Chapter 1

HE SENT HIS WORD AND HEALED THEM

Psalm 107:20 says, *"He sent His word, and healed them, and delivered (them) from their destructions."* Be excited that you are one of them. God's word brings healing. Acts 20:20 says, *"And now, brethren, I commend to you God, and to the word of His grace, which is able to build you up and to give you an inheritance among all them which are sanctified."* The word of God is designed to build you up, strengthen and heal you, also to bring wholeness, stability and deliverance, which is your inheritance as a child of God.

Now that you're in the family of God, expect and enjoy the family benefits. Psa. 119:50 says, *"This is my comfort in my affliction: for thy word hath quickened me, or has given and brought me life."* God's word comforts you and brings life to you when you are afflicted. As I stated earlier in the book, the word of God is like medicine, so just as you might take medicine two or three times a day, do the same with the promises in the word of God regarding healing. Rom. 10:17 says, *"So then faith comes by hearing, and hearing by the word of God."* Faith comes, strength comes, healing comes, deliverance comes by hearing the word of God. Go ahead; take your spiritual medicine, the word of God; it's going to make a huge difference in your life.

Prov. 4:20-22 says, *"Son, attend to my words: incline thine ear unto my saying, let them not depart from thine eyes, keep them in the mist of thine heart, for they are life unto those that find them and health (medicine) to all their flesh."* Just as you take your natural medicine prescribed by your doctor, add the word of God along with it. Prescribed medicine can heal and help some things, but God's word (spiritual medicine) can help all things. Think about it; no one has ever overdosed on Scriptures, so go ahead; take as many as you need, when you need them.

I used to work in the pharmacy and reading prescriptions can be hard. For example, the prescription *"tk 2 tab po tid prn"* means take 2 tablets by mouth 3 times a day as needed. However, most prescriptions don't have refills, without first seeing your doctor. But, with God there are unlimited refills. Whenever you need a word (medicine), pick up your Bible, attend Bible studies, or worship service at your local church. You should never run out of the word from God because He refills you every day as needed, praise God.

> Whenever you need a word (medicine) pick up your Bible

One of my favorite Scriptures comes from John 8:32, *"And ye shall know the truth and the truth shall make you free."* Once you know the truth concerning healing in God's word, then you can begin to exercise faith and expect the promises of God concerning healing for you. Jeremiah makes it so clear in chapter 23, verse 29, that God's word is like fire! *"Is not my word like fire? Says the Lord, and like a hammer that breaks the rock in pieces?"* This is a fact that all believers should get deep down in their heart: the word of God is an all-consuming fire, that will melt away and burn off whatever is not of God. I especially like this part; it's also a powerful crushing force that will break apart even the strongest and toughest circumstances.

I remember the movie *The Empire Strikes Back.* Well, it's time for the body of Christ to strike back; take the word of God and strike your situation until your situation gives up, gives way, breaks up, or breaks down, as the word says they should be. Think about it; the word of God will burn up everything or melt away the power of the enemy. God's word has a lot more power than we think. John 6:63 says, *"It is the spirit who gives life, the flesh profits nothing, the words that I speak unto you they are spirit and they are life."* God's word brings healing and life to your flesh.

If you were driving from Los Angeles to Chicago, you would have to fill up your vehicle with fuel more than just once, so traveling through this lifelong journey, we should continue to fill up on the word of God, and not let our spirit become empty. As we would stop at a gas station to fuel our vehicle, and would ask the attendant to fill up our gas tank, know within yourself that you have many miles ahead of you. It is important that you don't forget there are many miles ahead of you in the rhythm of the spirit, so fill up daily; you have many miles left.

John 15:7 says, *"If you abide in me and my words abide in you, you will ask what you desire, and it shall be done for you."* It's important to note that there is something that you must do, and that is you must abide or remain stable or fixed, to continue in a place, and also let the word abide in you; then you can ask what you desire, but your first desire should be to continue in the word of God. Isa. 55:11 says, *"So shall my word be that go forth out of my mouth, it shall not return unto me void (empty), but it shall accomplish that which I please, and it shall prosper in the things whereto I sent it."*

God's healing will be accomplished in you through His word. Jer. 1:12 says, *"Then said the Lord unto me, thou hast well seen; for I will hasten my word to perform it."* God is actively watching over His word to perform it; He's searching eagerly for someone like you to take Him at

His word so that He can perform it on your behalf. Wow, it is a blessing to know in Josh. 21:45 that there failed not ought of any good thing which the Lord had spoken unto the house of Israel: all came to pass, glory be to God, and because of the shed blood of Jesus Christ, we are in covenant with God so therefore the promises shall come to pass.

2

GOD GAVE ME A YES!

"For all the promises of God in Him are yes, and in Him, Amen, unto the glory of God by us."

2 CORINTHIANS 1:20

Chapter 2

GOD GAVE ME A YES!

It's wonderful and exciting to know God is a promise keeper! *"For all the promises of God in Him are yes, and in Him, Amen, unto the glory of God by us"* (2 Cor. 1:20). Hallelujah! He has given us a yes! Psa. 30:2 says, *"O Lord my God, I cried unto thee, and thou hast healed me."* I found also in the word of God that John 6:37 says, *"All that the Father giveth to me I will in no wise cast out."* So, come to God; you're His child and He wants to heal you!

Psa. 107:19-20 says, *"Then they cry unto the Lord in their trouble, and he saveth them out of their distresses. He sent his word, and healed them, and delivered them from their destructions."* God's word is the key to deliverance and distress in your life, so use your keys to unlock what is promised to you! Matt. 7:7-8 says, *"Ask, and it shall be given to you, seek, and you will find, knock, and it will be opened to you. For everyone who asks receives, and he who seeks finds, and to him who knocks it will be opened."* God longs to distribute what He has to the one in need. The word **ask** in the Greek means asking in faith, knowing that what you request of God, belongs to you! When you know that you are entitled to God's healing, according to His word, it's easy to ask. So, ask God; it's yours.

1 John 5:14-15 is one of my favorite Scriptures; it says, *"Now this is the confidence that we have in him, that if we ask anything according to his will, he hears us, and if we know that he hears us, whatsoever we ask, we know that we have the petitions that we have asked of him."* The word of God is the will of God. If we can find it in the word of God, then you can be confident that it is the will of God. The Lord is not trying to keep healing from us; He is trying to get it to us. Ask Him and believe! *"Let them shout for joy and be glad, who favor my righteous cause; and let them say continually. Let the Lord be magnified, who has pleasure in the prosperity of his servants"* (Psa. 35:27).

> The Lord is not trying to keep healing from us; He is trying to get it to us

This Scripture not only refers to prosperity in wealth, the word in the Hebrew for prosperity here is "shalom" and we know it as the word peace. However, in the Hebrew, this word literally means health, prosperity, peace, wholeness, missing nothing, lacking nothing. So, we can clearly see the mind of God who takes pleasure in the health, wholeness, prosperity, and peace of his children! God is just as excited to give healing to us as we are to receive it. Once you get the revelation of this, praise and adoration will flow through you like a mighty river, for which God is to us, and what He has already done through us. Doubt will no longer have a stronghold in your thinking. Praise God.

Paul the Apostle said in 2 Cor. 1:15-20, *"Because I was sure of this, I wanted to come to you first, so that you might have a double pleasure. I wanted to visit you on my way to Macedonia, and to come back to you from Macedonia and have you send me on my way to Judaea was I hesitating when I wanted to do this? Do I make my plans like a worldly man, ready to say yes and no at once?*

"As surely as God is faithful, our word to you has not been, yes and no, for the son of God, Jesus Christ, whom we preached among you, Silvanus and Timotheus and I, was not yes and no, but in Him it is always yes, for all the promises of God find their yes in Him. That's why we say amen through Him, to the glory of God." The question that I would like to ask you is, have you said yes to all of God's yes to you?

Is there any of God's yes to you to which you are saying no or maybe not now? Let our consecration to God from this point on be yes—yes to you, O God. I consecrate myself to forsake the no and the maybe and not concerning this wherever and whenever and however God is saying yes to me in my life.

Lord, I say yes to everything in your yes to me. Yes to your will and yes to your way. God never said to the world, no, to sending His son Jesus to die for the sins of the world. He didn't say maybe; no way! God gave the world a yes.

The Bible says in Rom. 8:32, *"He that spared not His own son, but delivered Him up for us all, how shall He not with Him also freely give us all things?"* When God gave us His only begotten son, He gave us a yes! God wants our yes to agree with His yes for our life.

God's heart is yes; God's heart is not divided toward you. God loves us constantly and not the next day maybe, or maybe not. God is consistent. He loves you continually, with your mistakes, flaws and all.

If you belong to Christ by faith, then everything God could possibly give to you for your good, He has signed over to your account in Christ. The question that might be asked is this: Is salvation a promise in my account? Yes. Is healing a promise in my account? Yes. Is deliverance a promise in my account? Yes. Is prosperity a promise in my account? Yes, yes, yes, yes!

All the promises of God are yes in Christ. Paul wrote in Gal. 3:29, *"If you are in Christ then you are Abraham's seed, and heirs according to His promise."*

His yes is not just for the believers; it is for sinners also that come to God in Christ. God comes to them in Christ with all of His promises. When a sinful person meets the Holy God in Christ, he hears a Yes, do you love me? Yes, will you forgive me? Yes, will you accept me? Yes, will you help me change? Yes, will you give me power to serve you? Yes, will you keep me? Yes, will you guide my path? Yes, will you show me your glory? Yes, yes, yes.

All the promises of God—all the blessings of God in heavenly places are yes in Christ Jesus. Jesus is God's decisive yes to all who believe.

In 2 Cor. 1:20, Paul said (all) the promises of God in Him are yes, and in Him amen, unto the glory of God by us. Verse 20 explains why the Church says "amen." It's a word taken over into the Greek from Hebrew, where it means "a very strong affirmation, a formal, solemn, earnest." I agree or I affirm what you just said, or this is true.

Amen means a very earnest yes in addressing God. If you notice, there is a connection between the two halves of verse 20. The first half says, *"For all the promises of God, finds their yes in Him."* The second half says, *"that is why we say amen through Him to God for His glory."* So, it is safe to say that amen and yes mean the same thing.

In Jesus Christ, God says His yes, His amen to us through His promises, and in Christ we say our yes, our amen back to God, through prayer, so go ahead and say yes to all God's promises to you, or amen to all of His promises.

So, when you say amen to what God's word says, you're saying yes, Lord, You can do it. Yes, Lord, You're all powerful. Yes, Lord, You are wise. Yes, Lord, You are merciful. Amen is like an exclamation point of faith in a statement of God's greatness.

As I stated earlier, let's consecrate ourselves to forsaking the no, and the maybe, and the not now, of unbelief, and say yes to everything in God's yes to us. Let's start right now! Yes, right now, God is waiting for your yes. He has already given us a yes in Christ Jesus, so every day start by saying this prayer: "God, in Jesus name, I say yes to your promise for my life, in Jesus' name, amen."

Say yes to all God's promises to you. Say amen to all of His promises!

3

DON'T TELL ME IT'S TOO LATE

"And Jesus looking upon them saith, with men it is impossible, but not with God, for with God all things are possible."

MARK 10:27

Chapter 3

DON'T TELL ME IT'S TOO LATE

When I found out that I had colon cancer, it was Stage 3! *"And Jesus looking upon them saith, with men it is impossible, but not with God, for with God all things are possible"* (Mark 10:27). See also Luke 1:37. Regardless of what men might say, trust in the Lord and lean not on your own understanding (Prov. 3:5-6). God specializes in things that are impossible; man's extremities are God's opportunities. When men go as far as they can go, then God steps in and does what man can't do.

Don't tell me it's too late!

In John 11:32-45, when Mary was come where Jesus was, and saw him, she fell down at his feet, saying unto him, *"Lord, if thou hadst been here, my brother had not died."* Even after four days and a stinking corpse, it's never too late for God. Jesus prayed to the Father and then cried out with a loud voice, *"Lazarus, come forth!"* And, at His word, Lazarus, who was dead, came forth alive.

Don't tell me it's too late!

Luke 8:49-55 tells the story of Jairus' daughter. *While he (Jesus) yet spake, there cometh one from the ruler of the synagogue's house, saying to him, "(Jairus), thy daughter is dead: trouble not the master." But, when Jesus heard it, he answered him, saying, "Fear not; believe only, and she shall be made whole."* It's so important not to say what you hear from the evil one; you must trust and believe only what the Lord says and meditate on what God's word says about your situation. Jesus later had everyone to leave the house except for Peter, James, John, the father and mother of the maiden. You might have to sanctify yourself or separate yourself from unbelievers, while you're trusting God for what you believe.

> Trust, believe and meditate only on what God's word says about your situation

Don't tell me it's too late!

Luke 8:43-47 records the story of a woman with an issue of blood. *"And the woman having an issue of blood 12 years, which had spent all her living upon physicians, couldn't be healed but got worse, came behind Jesus, and touched the border of his garment, and immediately her issue of blood dried up."* She had had this issue for 12 long years! I don't know how long you've had your issue, but God is not intimidated by how long you've had your issue, or by your issue itself. God is all powerful, so don't let your issue or circumstance keep you from trusting the Lord, for He is Jehovah-Rapha, your healer.

Don't tell me it's too late!

John 9:1-11 tells the story of a blind man. *"And as Jesus passed by, he saw a man which was blind from his birth."* Jesus sees your situation and circumstances, and He knows and cares all about them. Jesus told the blind man to go, wash in the pool of Siloam which is by interpretation, *sent*, and when the blind man trusted and obeyed His word and washed, he came away seeing. The key to this blind man's healing was that he first trusted what Jesus said, then he did what Jesus said. James 2:26 says, *"For as the body without the spirit is dead, so faith without works is dead also."*

Don't tell me it's too late!

The disciples asked Jesus, saying, *"Master, who did sin, this man or his parents that he was born blind?"* Jesus said, *"Neither, but that the works of God should be made manifest in him."* His neighbors asked, *"Are you the same man that was blind?"* and He said, *"I am he."* They asked, *"How did your eyes open?"* He said, a man that is called Jesus healed me. Testifying is so important, and letting others know of the goodness of God. So, go ahead and share what the Lord has done for the world, and for you. Amen!

And ... don't tell me it's too late!

4 GOD'S BENEFIT PACKAGE

"Blessed be the Lord, who daily loaded us with benefits, even the God of our salvation."

PSALM 68:19

Chapter 4

GOD'S BENEFIT PACKAGE

Just like on a 9-5 job, you look forward to knowing what's in your benefit package. There's life insurance, medical insurance, 401k investments, paid vacations, dental insurance and also, if you have a family, they are included. Accepting God as your Lord and Savior also has its benefits, such as healing, deliverance, peace, protection, grace, mercy, wealth, and favor. This is exciting to know that this is in your benefit package as a born-again believer. We are loaded with these benefits daily. *"Blessed be the Lord, who daily loaded us with benefits, even the God of our salvation"* (Psa. 68:19).

You are entitled to healing; it's in your benefit package (Bible). Open it up and read it. Your spiritual benefit is the word of God. He wants you to know what's promised to you so you can live a whole or complete life in Christ. What is important for believers to know is that our spiritual benefits never change; they're the same yesterday, today and forevermore. What I love about these benefits is they are not given to you because of your goodness, but because of the goodness of God.

What makes God's benefits so wonderful is you don't have to wait 4-6 months before the full benefits kick in. As soon as you accept God as your Lord and Savior, your benefits start right away. Furthermore, the benefits of God are transferable, so whereever you go – out of the city, state or country – as long as you stay connected to God, your benefits are in effect. Jer. 29:11 says, *"'For I know the thoughts that I think toward you,' says the Lord, 'thoughts of peace and not evil, to give you a future and a hope (an expected end).'"*

Again, the word for peace here in the Hebrew is *shalom* and implies the meaning of health and prosperity, which is obviously His will as it is regarding the end or goal that the Lord is expecting for us. So, begin to expect it; yes, my brother and my sister, I'm talking to you! Expect it! That's right; get your hopes up. I mean, get them way up! God is getting ready to give you the end or goal that He is expecting for you, so get excited and raise your hope to another level in the Lord. Remember, God's thoughts are peaceful toward you and not evil.

Don't allow your sickness, pain, or feelings to make you think that God is not having peaceful thoughts toward you. Sometimes your feeling and pain will make you think that God doesn't love you or He's angry with you; that is so far from the truth. Isa. 55:7 says, *"Let the wicked forsake his way, and the unrighteous man his thoughts and let him return to the Lord, and he will have mercy upon him; and to our God, for he will abundantly pardon."*

Verses 8-11 of that chapter continue, *"For my thoughts are not your thoughts, neither are your ways my ways, saith the Lord, for as the heavens are higher than the earth, so are my ways higher than your ways, for as the rain cometh down, and the snow from heaven and returned not thither, but watereth the earth, and maketh it to bring forth and bud, that it may give seed to the sower, and bread to the eater. So shall my word be that goeth forth out of my mouth; it shall not return unto me void, but it shall accomplish that which I please, and it shall prosper in the things whereto I sent it."*

Let me encourage you that God loves you with an everlasting love (Jer. 31:3). Rom. 5:8 says: *"But God commendeth his love toward us, in that, while we were yet sinners, Christ died for us."* While you're trusting God, continue to meditate on the word of God concerning your healing so that fear will not set in. The Bible says in 2 Tim. 1:7, *"For God hath not given us the spirit of fear; but of power, and of love and of a sound mind."* The enemy of our souls, satan, comes to steal, kill and destroy, to steal your joy, peace, and your faith so he can destroy your confidence in God, but the Lord said, *"I am come that you might have life and have it more abundantly."* One part of abundant life in Christ Jesus is good health.

In Luke 12:32, it says, *"Do not fear, little flock, for it is your father's good pleasure to give you the kingdom."* Along with the kingdom, comes all of the kingdom blessings and kingdom benefits! My brother, my sister, it's important to know that God wants us to realize that it gives God good pleasure to give to you! God is a giver, and He is love, and love gives. So, cast your cares upon Him, for He careth for you! The book of Psalms shares with us that in our benefit package, you will learn that God is a keeper; in the mist of your storms in life, He will keep you in perfect peace, if your mind is stayed on him (Isa. 26:3).

> God is a giver—it gives Him good pleasure to give to you!

Psa. 121:7-8 says, *"The Lord shall preserve (keep) you from all evil; He shall preserve your soul (life). The Lord shall preserve your going out and your coming in from this time forth and even forevermore."* God said He would keep or preserve you from all evil so surely that includes sickness and disease. The word for preserve means to guard, to keep you now and forevermore. That's right; praise the Lord. Go ahead right where you are! God is a keeper, so let me encourage you, no matter what the enemy says concerning your health, he is a liar because *"greater is he that is in you than he that in the world"* (1 John 4:4). The book of Hebrews teaches us that the Lord God will also make you perfect or equipped, to do whatever He needs you to do for His kingdom, which is in you, that which is well pleasing in His sight through Jesus Christ, which includes healing, prosperity, and wholeness. God wants us to have good health and wholeness so we can accomplish His will without any hindrance.

Being loaded with benefits daily, should help you to believe that loving, serving and living a godly lifestyle pays off — both in this life, and in the life to come. Just think about it; daily, every day, God is releasing protection, favor, prosperity, and deliverance. It's yours; this is the heart of the Father toward us. If we don't realize them today, God loads us up again the next day, then the next, and so on. Let's not forget that our benefits are connected to our salvation. Salvation has to be first and foremost in our lives. Matt. 6:33 says, *"But seek ye first the kingdom of God, and his righteousness, and all these things shall be added unto you"* (including healing).

Let's talk about these things for a moment; as a believer, you want different things in life – houses, cars, jobs, clothes, jewelry, tools, furniture, appliances, etc., but, God wants you to have salvation first. Think about it; healing is part of God's benefit package, but sickness is not, so don't receive it. Parents always say to their children: if a stranger offers you something, don't take it, because it might cost you your life. Satan is the stranger, so don't accept anything from him. He's not your heavenly Father, and he wants to offer you sickness AND everything in the family of sickness, but whatever is your Father's (God's) is part of your benefit package, praise God.

5

HEALING IS A GIFT FROM GOD

"Every good gift and every perfect gift is from the Father of lights, with whom is no variableness, neither shadow of turning."

JAMES 1:17

Chapter 5

HEALING IS A GIFT FROM GOD

Scripture says, *"Every good gift and every perfect gift is from the Father of lights, with whom is no variableness, neither shadow of turning"* (Jas. 1:17). One of the best gifts we can receive from God is healing. What is so wonderful about that is, God never changes; what He did yesterday, He will do again today, and forevermore.

I'm so thankful that He is still the healer of the mind, body and the soul. Praise the Lord. Unlike people who might give someone something, and then out of anger, want to take it back, praise God that *"the gifts and calling of God are without repentance,"* or are irrevocable (Rom. 11:29). Our God is a giver of gifts and He doesn't take them back, and they cannot be canceled! *"For it is God who works in you, both to will and to do for his good pleasure"* (Phil. 2:13).

Worship is a key to intimacy with God and it will also help you to experience God's rest. Matt. 11:28 says, *"Come unto me, all ye that labor and are heavy laden, and I will give you rest."* Worship brings you into God's presence so that our soul might experience relief and ease. The word "rest" means to cease from toil, struggle, and labor in order to recover and collect one's strength. Our responsibility is to place our focus onto Jesus and not on our circumstances, and begin to praise God for what He has done for us. Spend more time each day just loving on God rather than complaining.

Deut. 29:29 says, *"The secret things belong to the Lord our God: but those things which are revealed belong unto us and to our children forever, that we may do all the words of this law."* It's wonderful to know that healing and health belong to you and your children and your family line. This has been revealed to us in the word of God, and comes through a blood covenant that we have in Jesus Christ. Remember, healing is in your benefit package, no matter what the enemy said to you or how the enemy tries to make you feel.

Refuse to let go of your birthright! Scripture makes it clear that healing belongs to you, so decree it and declare it over your life daily. Go ahead and say it: it's mine, it's mine, healing is mine. 1 Cor. 3:21-22 says, *"Therefore let no man glory in men, for all things present, or things to come; all are yours."* Go ahead and say it again; it's mine.

What is a gift? A gift is something given voluntarily without payment in return, as to show favor toward someone, or make a gesture of assistance.

Healing is a gift from God to show His love toward us, without payment from us. Even though it is free to us, it doesn't mean it came cheap; Jesus paid a very high price for our healing.

Jesus is a gift from God who voluntarily came to the earth to redeem man. Psa. 107:1-2 says, *"O give thanks unto the Lord, for He is good, for His mercy endureth forever. Let the redeemed of the Lord say so, whom He hath redeemed from the hand of the enemy."*

God gives us the gift of healing because it's His nature to save and heal. 1 John 3:8 says, *"...For this purpose the Son of God was manifested that He might destroy the works of the devil"* (sickness, disease, illness).

The Bible says, *"Every good and perfect gift is from above, and cometh down from the Father of light with whom is no variableness, neither shadow of turning"* (Jas. 1:17). The NIV translation says, *"Every good and perfect gift is from above, coming down from the Father of heavenly lights, who does not change like shifting shadows."* Even though your circumstances change, God will never change. Heb. 13:8 says, *"Jesus is the same yesterday and today and forevermore."* If He healed back then, He will do the same today.

I remember when my son was about four years old. His birthday was just a few days away. He kept reminding me that in a few days he would be five years old. He also reminded me of what gift he wanted and what I had promised him. He didn't know that I didn't have any money and I wasn't working at the time, but I had a very expensive watch that I pawned, and traded the watch in for cash.

Even though the watch was expensive, my love for my son was priceless, I was able to give my son the best birthday he ever had. I watched my son jump around excited about the gift that he received. I was more excited to give the gift than he was to receive it.

> Keep reminding God of what He promised in His word ...

What my son did was kept reminding me over and over what I had promised him for his birthday, so keep reminding God of what He promised in His word concerning healing and watch God come through for you.

Matt. 7:8-11 says, *"For everyone that asketh receiveth and he that seeketh findeth, and to Him that knocketh it shall be opened. Or what man is there of you, whom if His son ask (for) bread, will He give him a stone? Or if he ask (for) a fish, will he give him a serpent. If ye being evil, know how to give good gifts unto your children, how much more shall your Father which is in heaven give good things to them that ask Him?"* Go ahead! God is waiting for you to ask Him, but you must ask in faith believing that it is God's will for your healing.

Heb. 11:6 says, *"But without faith it is impossible to please Him, for He that cometh to God must believe that He is and that He is a rewarder of them that diligently seek Him.* Heb. 10:23 says, *"Let us hold fast the profession of our faith without wavering, for He is faithful that promised."*

So, remember that healing is a gift that God promised to all believers.

I remember a funny story that happened to my brother and I over 25 years ago. We both worked together for a pharmaceutical company where we delivered medication to a senior citizen nursing facility that was in the far suburbs. After dropping off the medication, it began to get dark very fast. There were no lights on the roads, our company car was almost on empty, and we had about 45 minutes to get home.

So, we found a gas station and pulled over to buy gas. I asked my brother, "How much should I put in the tank?"

He yelled, "Fill 'er up," so I did.

After about five minutes, my brother walked towards the car like he had seen a ghost, and asked me, "How much did it cost to fill up the tank?"

Not understanding his concern I said, "Forty-five dollars, why? We have the company fuel card to purchase the gas."

My brother shook his head and replied, "We are in big trouble."

"Why?" I asked.

"I just tried to pay for the gas at an Amoco station, with a Shell gas card!" he answered.

Between the two of us, we had only three dollars in cash. This was not a good situation.

The clerk was about to call the police. I apologized over and over, but she said. "Sorry is not going to pay for the gas," so I asked to call my supervisor. She said, "Yes, but you only get one call and the police will be here in two minutes." I called my supervisor and told him what had happened, and he said, "Put the clerk on the line." After three minutes she hung up the phone and said, "You guys are so lucky." I asked, "What did he say?" She said, "He charged what you owed to his account, on his credit card." We got back into our car and drove home, thanking and praising God all the way.

This reminded me of Phil. 1:18, *"If He hath wronged thee, or owed thee ought, put it on mine account."* Let me encourage you. God has already paid for our healing on the cross; He charged it to His account.

Isa. 53:4-5 says, *"Surely He hath borne our griefs and carried our sorrows, yet we did esteem Him stricken of God and afflicted, but He was wounded for our transgressions. He was bruised for our iniquities. The chastisement of our peace was upon Him and with His stripes we are healed."* So, go ahead and celebrate your healing. It's a gift from God. Don't let what you hear, see or feel, stop you from believing what God's word says.

Don't let
what you
hear, see or
feel, stop
you from
believing
what God's
word says

6

GOD CANNOT LIE

"God is not a man, that he should lie ..."

NUMBERS 23:19a

Chapter 6

GOD CANNOT LIE

God is not a man. He does not make mistakes. *"God is not a man, that he should lie: neither the son of man, that he should repent: hath he said, and shall he not do it? Or hath he spoken, and shall he not make it good?"* (Num. 23:19). He doesn't make promises that He can't keep. If the Lord said it, He's going to do what He said in His word. Our responsibility is to confess what God's word says about healing, and then believe what the word of God says. Once you confess, then believe and you'll receive what is promised to you in God's word, concerning healing, deliverance, and prosperity. Rejoice in knowing that all of the promises of God in Him are yes and in Him amen unto the glory of God by us (2 Cor. 1:20).

Because God is not a man, He is not limited to any supplies that you might need. The Scripture says, *"But my God shall supply all your need according to his riches in glory by Christ Jesus"* (Phil. 4:19). Being a man, even doctors, pharmacists, and nurses are limited to supplies of medicine to help bring healing to the body, but our Lord and Savior Jesus Christ, not only has supplies for your body, but for your mind and your soul. There is no limit to what God can and will do if you believe.

> If you know the word of God, then you know the will of God

Heb. 10:23 says, *"Let us hold fast to the profession of (our) faith without wavering: (for he is) faithful that promised."* It's impossible for God to lie, and since God can't lie, the Bible says that we should have confidence in Him. 1 John 5:14-15 says, *"Now this is the confidence that we have in him, that if we ask anything according to his will. He hears us, and if we know that he hears us whatever we ask, we know that we have the petition that we have asked of him."* It's easy to know the will of God when you know the word of God.

It's wonderful to know I don't have to worry when the Lord watches over His word to perform it. Therefore, ask, believe and receive as long as it is in the word of God, and is in the will of God, so in knowing this, my faith shall increase and my confidence shall not be cast away, because I'm believing to receive His great reward (Heb. 10:35-36).

God cannot lie, because that's not His nature, and God can't go against His own nature. The Bible says in John 14:6, *"I am the way, the truth and the life; no man cometh unto the Father, but by me."*

God cannot lie because He is consistent. He doesn't say one thing and do another, unlike man. They would say one thing and forget they said it, or say they will do something and never get around to doing what they say they are going to do.

God is not like man; He cannot lie. If He said He's going to do something, He will. God can't abandon you or not care – He is going to be there for you. He will be there to meet your needs, because His word is true in Heb. 13:5 *"... I will never leave thee, nor forsake thee."*

Whatever God says to you in His word is truth; it's not a lie. He can't lie; that's not part of His DNA. We are wired with certain DNA that makes us human and makes us the individual that we are. Our DNA gives us certain characteristics and traits.

You can't change your DNA. You can pretend, by putting dye in your hair if you like, to color it black, blonde, or green. You can even put different color contacts in your eyes; you can even bleach your skin. Some have even had operations to change their lifestyle, but their DNA, is still the same.

You can't change who you really are; if so, you're just pretending. I'm so thankful that God is not pretending to be God. God is God and everything about Him is true.

When Jesus said in John 12: 32 *"... and if I be lifted up from the earth, will draw all men unto me."* God didn't lie; He's drawing men unto Him every minute of every hour.

But, there is one the Bible calls the Father of lies, the deceiver, the devil; now, he can't help but lie; that's a part of his DNA. He has been lying ever since creation. Remember how he lied to Eve in the Garden of Eve. He's still lying today. He would deceive you into doing something wrong and then say, "How could you? I can't believe you did that. God will never forgive you for that. You're a failure. You are pathetic. You're not saved. God is done with you! You'll never get a job; you'll never finish school; you'll never get delivered from that; you'll never get healed." Because satan is a liar, he always tries to deceive you by telling you the opposite of what God says.

God is not like the devil. He would never say those words to you. When God made a promise to Abraham, since there was no one greater for Him to swear by, He swore by Himself, saying, "I will surely bless you and give you many descendants."

God promised at an old age Abraham and Sarah would have a son. God did not lie. They had Isaac. The promise that Abraham would be blessed with many descendants is still happening now. It's wonderful to know that we are not holding on to a lie from God that might break, when things get too heavy in our lives. We can hold onto God's promises, because they are true and not a lie.

Because Jesus Christ lived a perfect life on the earth, and because He died, was buried and resurrected, God's promises are fulfilled.

You might ask what the promises are. Well, God said He will save you. This frees you from worrying about the future.

You don't have to worry about what comes after death. God will save you because He promised and He can't lie. God said He will forgive you. God has promised that He would wipe your slate clean of all your past mistakes. He'll remember your sins no more.

You might ask what this does? It frees you from shame, from regret in your life so you don't have to feel crippled. You don't have to drag guilt around any longer because He can't lie.

> Since God can't lie to us, we can trust His motives

God also promises to give you direction in life. So, you won't have to stumble around in life wondering which way to go, or how am I going to get there. God will give you guidance and direction in life. God promises His Holy Spirit to guide you and we know He can't lie.

These promises can be used as a guide for the rest of your life, like a compass to make sure you're heading in the right direction.

Since God can't lie to us, we can trust His motives; His motives are good. I think we have seen enough and know enough about relationships, that there must be trust to have a good relationship.

The Bible says in Prov. 3:5-6, *"Trust in the Lord with all thine heart and lean not to thine own understanding; in all thy ways, acknowledge Him, and He shall direct thy paths."* And that's a promise you can count on.

Since God will never lie to us, we can rest in His truth. Jesus says in John 14:6, *"I am the way, the truth and the life."* He didn't say, I stand for the truth, or I represent the truth. He said, *"I am the truth."* Jesus Christ is God and He loves us and He will never lie to us. And that's the truth.

God loves you unconditionally, with your mistakes, flaws and all, and that's no lie. God loves you more than you love yourself, and that's no lie.

God will keep you in perfect peace, if you keep your mind on Him, and that's no lie. God's word says, *"Give and it shall be given unto you, pressed down shaken together and running over shall men give unto you."* And, that's no lie.

God's word says that He's a healer, and that's no lie.

God cannot lie. Psa. 103:2-3 says, *"Praise the Lord, O my soul, and forget not all His benefits—who forgiveth (all) thine iniquities, who healeth all thy diseases."*

God cannot lie. Psa. 107:20 says, *"He sent His word, and healed them, and delivered them from their destructions,"* and that's no lie.

God cannot lie. Psa. 46:1 says, *"God is our refuge and strength, a very present help in trouble,"* and that's no lie.

God cannot lie. Psa. 91:16 says, *"With long life will I satisfy Him and show Him my salvation,"* and that's no lie.

God cannot lie. Jer. 30:17 says, *"For I will restore health unto them, and heal thee of thy wounds, saith the Lord."* So, let me encourage you. God cannot and will not lie, because He is the truth! Amen.

7

HOW TO RECEIVE YOUR HEALING

"If ye abide in me, and my words abide in you, ye shall ask what ye will, and it shall be done unto you."

JOHN 15:7

Chapter 7

HOW TO RECEIVE YOUR HEALING

Knowing what's rightfully yours is very important! You need to understand that, as a child of God, you are fully entitled to your healing; it's part of your benefit package from God through the blood that Jesus shed on the cross at Calvary. By His stripes we are already healed. Remember, if you don't know it's God's will that you are healed, then you're going to lack what's important, which is faith. Without faith it is impossible to please God, because faith is how we receive what Christ did for us. Remember, when you were first saved, it was by faith that you received Christ into your heart. The same is true for healing; it's by faith that we receive the promises of God. 1 Cor. 1:20 says, *"For the promises of God in him are yes and in him, Amen"* unto the glory of God by us.

REPENT FROM SIN

Repent of any unconfessed sins. 1 John 1: 8-9 says, *"If we say that we have no sin, we deceive ourselves, and the truth is not in us."* Rom. 3:23 adds, *"For all have sinned and fall short of the glory of God."* If we confess our sins, He is faithful and just to forgive us of our sins and cleanse us from all unrighteousness! Unconfessed sins can be sins that have been lingering for years and not addressed to God; we need to confess and forsake our sins, because when we do, God graciously forgives us. Cleanse us from them, O Lord, so they won't block our healing.

FORGIVE

Do you have any unforgiveness in your heart? If so, release it! Unforgiveness will block your healing. If you are holding grudges or bitterness against someone, you need to release that, because it will block your healing. If when you see someone that hurt you and it still bothers you, or when you think of someone who hurt you and it still bothers you, it's time to give those feelings to the Lord, and leave them there. Unforgiveness can come between you and God and prevent your own sins from being forgiven, so release it!

If you truly want to be healed from infirmities, sickness, and disease, you must decide today to release those hurts and feelings to God in prayer. Forgiveness is a choice, so go ahead and make that choice, not to let unforgiveness keep you in bondage any longer. When you make that choice, ask God to help you to heal and release everyone that hurt you and/or those you love. Let's pray now:

> Father God, in the name of Jesus, I have been holding on to bitterness and unforgiveness in my heart against ______________________________ because of what they did to me or said about me, or someone I love or care about, and I repent for not forgiving them as you have commanded me. Forgive me for not forgiving them as I know I should have. I now in the name of Jesus release those hurts and feelings to you; I renounce and break agreement with bitterness and unforgiveness, and I freely choose to forgive them now. Amen!

AGREE WITH WHAT GOD SAYS

We have the privilege and authority to touch and agree in prayer about any situation or issue. *"Again I say unto you, That if two of you shall agree on earth as touching anything that they shall ask, it shall be done for them of my Father which is in heaven"* (Matt. 18:19). Another way which can help your healing to manifest, is when another believer, who is strong in faith, agrees with you by the laying on of hands. Just remember, it's not them healing you, it's God working through them. *"Again I say unto you, That if two of you shall agree on earth as touching anything that they shall ask, it shall be done for them of my Father which is in heaven"* (Mark 16:17-18).

SPEAK WORDS OF FAITH

"The words that I speak unto you, they are spirit, and they are life" (John 6:63b). Speak the word of faith over yourself and others, because you have been given that authority to do so, to be healed and to heal. So, start today; speak to that part of your body that needs healing and command it to be healed in Jesus name! Jesus said in John 14:12, *"Verily, verily, I say unto you, He that believeth on me, the works that I do shall he do also; and greater works than these shall he do; because I go unto my Father."*

Jesus also said in John 5:8 that *"Jesus saith unto him, Rise, take up thy bed, and walk."* Acts 3:6 records, *"Then Peter said, Silver and gold have I none; but such as I have give I thee: In the name of Jesus Christ of Nazareth rise up and walk."*

DO NOT DOUBT

"And immediately Jesus stretched forth his hand, and caught him, and said unto him, O thou of little faith, wherefore didst thou doubt?" (Matt. 14:31).

Lack of faith is truly a blockage that can prevent healing; Jesus made it clear in many healings that faith is important for you to receive your healing. Matt. 9:29 says, *"Then touched he their eyes, saying, According to your faith be it unto you."* Jesus touched their eyes, saying according to your faith be it unto you, and it was so. Also, Matt. 9:22 tells us, *"But Jesus turned him about, and when he saw her, he said, Daughter, be of good comfort; thy faith hath made thee whole. And the woman was made whole from that hour."*

BELIEVE AND ASK

If you can believe, all things are possible to him that believes. Mark 11:24 says, *"Therefore I say unto you, what things so ever ye desire, when ye pray, believe that ye receive them, and ye shall have them."* A lack of faith can and will block us from receiving the Lord, but believing in His promises sets us up to receive them. Jas. 1:6-7 adds, *"But let him ask in faith, nothing wavering. For he that wavereth is like a wave of the sea driven with the wind and tossed. For let not that man think that he shall receive anything of the Lord."*

8 KEYS TO UNLOCK YOUR HEALING

"Death and life are in the power of the tongue: and they that love it shall eat the fruit thereof."

PROVERBS 18:21

Chapter 8

KEYS TO UNLOCK YOUR HEALING

Your keys are in your mouth. They won't show up on a dental exam because they come from the tongue, not the teeth. Prov. 18:21 says, *"Death and life are in the power of the tongue: and they that love it shall eat the fruit thereof."* So, let's talk about fruit. Most fruits have seeds, and the seeds are designed to reproduce the same fruit they came from. If you like the fruit and want more of that same fruit, just keep planting that seed. Similarly, if you like what the word of God is producing in your life, keep speaking or planting God's word into your life.

It's important to note that your healing is only a seed or a word away from being planted. It's amazing to know that we have that much power in our mouth. Therefore, if what is being produced in your life is not bringing life to you, stop saying it! And, start today, yes, right now and declare that you will speak God's life-giving words over and into your life and into the lives of others. Every morning start confessing that by speaking life over your health, wealth, marriage, children, ministry, job, church, neighborhood, town, city, state, and nation, and watch life start being produced over and through your life, praise the Lord.

Unlock your healing with the keys God has given you in His word. This is your year of open doors, but, remember, you have the keys.

They're in your mouth. Speak the word over it and into your situation, and watch doors open. Matt. 16:19 says that *"I will give unto thee the keys of the kingdom of heaven;"* and whatsoever thou shalt bind on earth or say no to on earth, He'll say no to in heaven, and whatsoever thou shalt loose on earth or say yes to on earth, He'll say yes to in heaven.

Therefore, satan can't bind you with sickness because you have the keys, the keys to healing deliverance, prosperity, and whatever else you need; it's in your mouth. If you look at Isa. 57:19 it also says, *"I create the fruit of the lips: peace to him that is far off, and to him that is near, saith the lord; and I will heal him."* Again, the word fruit here means produce.

God creates what you produce from your mouth when we believe and speak God's words out of our mouth. Believe it, your words are powerful; whatever you don't want to produce, then just don't say. Those things that you are believing God for such as healing, deliverance, and wealth—find God's words which relate to your situation and start saying what God's word says. Mark 11:24 reads, *"Therefore I say unto you, what things so ever ye desire, when ye pray, believe that ye receive (them) and ye shall have them."*

> Find God's words which relate to your situation and start saying them

If you would just go back two verses to Mark 11:22-23, this might help as well: *"And Jesus answering saith unto them, have faith in god, for verily I say unto you, that whosoever shall say unto this mountain, be thou removed, and be thou cast into the sea; and not doubt in his heart, but shall believe that those things which he saith shall come to pass; he shall have whatsoever he saith."*

What kind of obstacle, or mountains, do you have in your life now? All you have to do is obey the word that Jesus said and command those mountains of pain, disease, cancer, sickness of any kind, to go now, be thou removed in Jesus name. Jesus said you can have what you say, so go ahead, begin to call those things which are not as though they were; call your body whole, healed, and functional. That's right, keep calling it no matter how you feel; don't listen to fear or doubt; just listen to Jehovah Rapha (the Lord who heals). Speak the promises of God in His word, and lay claim to them as your inheritance. Don't forget, healing is part of your benefit package; therefore, decree that you are healed! Say this prayer:

> Lord, you said that by your stripes I am healed, so on the power and authority of Your word, I decree that I am healed and that sickness and diseases have no legal right or stronghold in me, because of my blood covenant that I have with Jesus. In the name of Jesus Christ, I am healed, delivered and set free. Amen.

Let the redeemed of the Lord say so! Testify of the goodness of the Lord. Psa. 107:2 says, *"Let the redeemed of the Lord say so, whom He hath redeemed from the hand of the enemy."* When your healing manifests itself and you recover and have the opportunity to testify to the grace of the Lord, then say it, tell it, do it. The Lord wants you to give glory to Him, for what He has done.

Your testimony will help others to build their faith in the Lord, for what they need in their life. Rev. 12:11 says, *"And they overcame him by the blood of the Lamb and by the word of their testimony."* Therefore, say it, tell it, go ahead and do it; someone is waiting to hear and see what the

Lord has done. After you've received the manifestation of your healing, this should be your stand of faith!

Nah. 1:7-9 says, *"The Lord is good, a stronghold in the day of trouble, and he knoweth them that trust in Him … What do ye imagine against the Lord? He will make an utter end and affliction shall not rise up the second time!"* Be healed, be delivered, be set free, in Jesus' name. Amen!

9 TESTIMONIES AS A RESULT OF THE HEALING

"And they overcame him by the blood of the Lamb and by the word of their testimony ..."

REVELATION 12:11a

Chapter 9

TESTIMONIES AS A RESULT OF THE HEALING

"And they overcame him by the blood of the Lamb and by the word of their testimony; and they loved not their lives unto the death." (Rev. 12:11)

"But none of these things move me, neither count I my life dear unto myself, so that I might finish my course with joy, and the ministry, which I have received of the Lord Jesus, to testify the gospel of the grace of God." (Acts 2:24)

"And we have seen and do testify that the Father sent the Son to be the Saviour of the world." (1 John 4:14)

"Now thanks be unto God, which always causeth us to triumph in Christ, and maketh manifest the savior of his knowledge by us in every place." (2 Cor. 2:14)

It has been over ten years now, after I have had surgery, radiation, and chemo treatments. The number ten in the Bible is symbolic of the perfection of divine order.

AS I LOOK BACK OVER MY LIFE

Apostle Dr. Eriq T. Harris, Sr.

I'm truly thankful to God for His perfect works and His perfect will being manifested in my life. God has shown himself strong on my behalf, because I believe God and according to Eph. 3:20 it says, *"Now unto him that is able to do exceeding abundantly above all that we ask or think, according to the power that worketh in us."* This has been a testament of God's awesome power; this has made my faith level in God to really increase to another level. Not only did I stand and believe God to heal my body physically, but healing me spiritually, emotionally and financially. For the word says in 3 John 1:2, *"Beloved, I wish above all things that thou mayest prosper and be in health, even as thy soul prospereth."* My faith in God's word has also encouraged me to believe God for healing, deliverance and finally, prosperity for others – both believers and non-believers.

What God did for me, wasn't just for me but for the benefit of those who don't believe. I know I can see the faith level in the most beautiful woman in the world, my wife, Pastor Lisa Harris. Not only did I see her believe God, through prayer and intercession for both family and friends, but for herself. A one hour outpatient surgery for multiple cysts on the uterus lasted over eight and a half hours. Upon the surgeon entering the waiting room, asking for the spouse, I almost thought the worst. God did not give me a spirit of fear. The doctor stated there was an accident; one of the uterine tubes was nicked and internal bleeding occurred. My response was, "FIX IT!" – not just to the doctor, but I began to speak to the Lord, and He did.

My children, church family, and pastoral friends, have seen God move on my behalf. It has been several years since my recovery, and some are still talking about what they have seen. The children, although young, were not too young to pray for their dad. From my oldest daughter, Brittany, and oldest son, Eriq Jr. down to Emanuel, Faith and Elijah, all have seen God move in their father's life. My mother's faith has grown as a result of my healing. I truly thank God for my wife, Lisa; if anyone knows what I've been through, she knows, so I'll never let a day go by and not realize that I am blessed.

I CALL HIM JEHOVAH-RAPHA

Lisa Harris—Wife of Apostle Eriq Harris

As I look back over the years, I thank God for all the wonderful things He has done. It has now been over ten years since my husband, Eriq Harris Sr., was first diagnosed with Stage 3 colon cancer. He stands today completely healed.

For the Bible says in Isa. 53:5, *"But he was* wounded for our transgressions, *he was* bruised for our iniquities: the chastisement of our peace *was* upon him; and with his stripes *we are healed*."

According to Strong's Concordance, healed in the Hebrew is translated to *rapha' (H7495)*, which means *cure, cause to heal, physician, repair thoroughly, make whole.*

Jehovah Rapha is one of the many names of the Lord. Jehovah is Yahweh, meaning Lord and master. Each name of God reveals something very important about Him, His nature and character. So, with knowing that Jehovah Rapha means healer, during the time of my husband's sickness, I called on Jehovah Rapha, The Lord God who heals you. Not only will Jehovah Rapha heal you physically but when you call upon His name, He will heal you emotionally and psychologically.

Nahum 1:9 says, *"What do ye imagine against the LORD? He will make an utter end: affliction shall not rise up the second time."* Affliction comes from the Hebrew word *tsarah* (Strong's H 6869), which translates to trouble, distress, adversity, anguish and tribulation.

During my husband's healing process, I had to walk by faith and not by sight. Faith in theology is the assent of the mind or understanding to the truth of what God has revealed. It is also simple belief of the Scriptures, of the being and perfection of God, and of the existence, character and doctrines of Christ, (King James Dictionary). My faith has truly increased. My faith received the healing. Seeing God manifest His healing power in my husband's life, actually prepared me for when I had to have surgery three years ago. My faith was not shaken. I was confident that the Lord would heal me and He did just that. The Bible talks about Jesus having compassion on the multitude of people. I laid my hand on the area that was not functioning properly and began to speak healing over my body! God has given me such a peace that when circumstances change, I'm able to remain calm and look towards heaven.

God will meet you right where you are. In your time with the Lord, talk with Him, if you are sick. The Lord is a healer, that He is. Victory belongs to Jesus! For I'm reminded in His word that 1 Pet. 2:24 says, *"Who his own self bare our sins in his own body on the tree that we, being dead to sins, should live unto righteousness: by whose stripes ye were healed."* Your healing has already been paid for, so I reminded God of His word. Nothing happens until you speak. Mark 11: 22-24 says, *"And Jesus answered them, "Have faith in God. Truly, I say to you, whoever says to this mountain, 'Be taken up and thrown into the sea,' and does not doubt in his heart, but believes that what he says will come to pass, it will be done for him. Therefore I tell you, whatever you ask in prayer, believe that you have received it, and it will be yours."*

After having seen God manifest his healing power, was there anything too hard for the Lord? No. When it was time to look for a location for Temple of Deliverance, we prayed and trusted God to guide us. He led us to a location which had been vacant for over 10 years, and God moved upon the heart of the owners to fix the building up for us without any money down on our part.

THE LORD INCREASED MY FAITH!

Betty Johnson—Maywood, Ill.

As a result of my apostle, Dr. Eriq T. Harris, Sr., receiving healing, my faith in God has been increased. I watched him as he went through treatments of chemotherapy and radiation. His physical appearance went through changes (darker and weight loss), but his spiritual being was elevated. He continued to trust God for his complete healing, while at the same time, praying for the people of God (Temple of Deliverance Church family) to stay together, which we did.

During his time of illness, I saw spiritual growth in our church as a whole. The members that stayed grew. I also saw spiritual growth in Pastor Lisa. She carried a heavy weight on her shoulder, but her trust and faith in God lifted that heavy burden from her. She was able to move forward in Jesus name and in His strength, and carry on the work of the church as if Apostle Harris was there.

As a result of being a witness to it all, my faith in God went to another level. I know what God can do. I've seen Him do it.

HEALED FROM DEPRESSION

Alexi L. Jackson - Chicago, Ill.

After hearing the testimony of the healing of Apostle Harris, I started to believe what God can do. I have been delivered from many things but one thing in particular I would like to mention. Mental illness is something that rarely gets talked about, but many people have dealt with it.

When I was 19 years old, I was diagnosed with Major Depressive Disorder. Growing up, I dealt with sexual, physical and emotional abuse and was bullied a lot. It got to the point that instead of talking to someone about it, I kept everything to myself.

I kept everything inside so much that I began to do self-harm to my own body. I would even threaten to commit suicide many times and actually came close to achieving that goal. At age 19, I was admitted to a mental institution. During this time, I had to get a medical withdrawal from the university, due to my being harmful to others and myself.

The psychiatrist and social worker helped me in many ways. I would take about four to five pills twice a day to help with the depression. There were medications such as Effexor XR and even Lithium. Over a 10-year span, I was also admitted to several mental institutions. A huge chunk of my life was taken away because of this.

There were times when I would get so frustrated that I would go in the bathroom and just cry, wanting my life to be over. Every time I would do this, I would hear a voice that would call my name. And every time, the Lord would bring to my remembrance why it was not my time to leave and that He needed me here for a reason. I did not know this at the time but, I had an angel watching over me despite the little faith I had in God.

In 2010, I became a member of Temple of Deliverance Life Changing Ministry where I rededicated my life back to the Lord and got back in the word. I would hear testimonies of healing and breakthroughs all the time. After hearing Apostle Harris's testimony, I knew that the same God could help me with this mental illness. I was to the point where I was tired of all the medication and going back and forth to counseling and I knew God had a plan for my life that did not consist of me not being in my right mind.

I began to respond to this illness by speaking positive affirmations in my life. There were times I felt discouraged because not everyone understood how important it was for me to get through this. Although people did not think I would overcome this illness, I still believed because I had begun to realize how much God loves me and wants a better life for me.

Before hearing Apostle Harris's testimony, I did not really have any faith. There was actually a time when I did not believe God. I had come a long way in my faith. I had begun to talk to God, letting Him know how I was tired of everything. It had taken me a while to get used to talking with God about anything because I never really trusted anyone growing up. I had begun to accept that I cannot even leave here until I do what He needs me to do. I eventually began to build a relationship with God. One Scripture that always stuck out to me was Rom. 8:28 which states, *"And we know that all things work together for good to them that love God, to them who are the called according to his purpose."* This became one of my favorite Scriptures. Whenever there was a time I thought I wasn't going to make it or felt like giving up, I would cite this Scripture.

Since 2011, I have not been on any medication. I was still seeing a counselor but now, my only counselor is God. I thank God every day for keeping me in my right mind.

If it was not for me coming to Temple of Deliverance Life Changing Ministries under the leadership of Apostle Eriq Harris, there is not any telling where I would be. I am delivered from Major Depressive Disorder and I no longer practice self-harm nor have suicidal thoughts. There are times where my mood would be off, but I do not let the devil get victory in it anymore. I thank God for how far He has brought and kept me and most of all for His grace, and for allowing me the opportunity to do His will.

HEALED FROM INTERNAL BLEEDING

Nicole Jackson—Chicago, Ill.

As a result of hearing the testimony of Pastor Lisa Harris, it helped me to become healed. I had lived for two years with bleeding and pain. I had gone to different doctors and no one knew what the issue was. Apostle Harris and Pastor Lisa have always told me how I need to speak positive words over my life. The doctors gave me several options for surgery. I was not in agreement with the idea of surgery at all. The doctors themselves were surprised at how much strength I had, with such a low blood count. In addition to the surgery, I was going to need a blood transfusion. A hysterectomy was performed. Prior to surgery, Apostle Harris called me for prayer and spoke healing over my life.

The day of surgery, the anesthesiologist came and explained the procedure of the surgery and how they would have blood on standby. All I can remember was what Apostle and Pastor told me which was that

God has the last say. Forty-five minutes later, surgery was over without any cutting. This was so amazing because I had never had surgery before. After knowing this, I was really praising God for who He is. I was fully recovered within two weeks. I truly thank God for Apostle Eriq and Pastor Lisa Harris along with Temple of Deliverance family for their testimonies and their healing process which has truly helped me through my different healing processes.

JOY OF HEALING!

Lila McKay—Chicago, Ill.

In the course of waiting to become and becoming a member of Temple of Deliverance, I would hear about when Pastor Harris had a sickness. I continued to listen and discovered that he was a cancer survivor. My membership in the ministry began to become even more precious to me. I felt so special to God because He had healed my Pastor (Apostle Harris) of cancer.

I can't imagine my life without Apostle Eriq T. Harris and Pastor Lisa Harris. God has spared his life, given him the victory over cancer and has used them mightily in our lives. They have been strength and help to us in so many ways. We were able to go to them when we needed a church home and they welcomed us as members. We went through a tough time in our marriage and they were there for us. We have been able to grow in grace and the knowledge of God from their preaching, teaching, and being examples of mature ministers of the Gospel of Jesus Christ. They have prayed for us, labored in the ministry diligently for us, spoken from the mouth of God to us, and been a father and mother to us.

10

HEALING SCRIPTURES AND CONFESSIONS

"If the Son therefore shall make you free, ye shall be free indeed."

JOHN 8:36

Chapter 10

HEALING SCRIPTURES AND CONFESSIONS

This chapter is dedicated to providing you with an easy reference for healing Scriptures and confessions you can speak out loud, meditate on, and memorize. Allow them to become your medicine—***God's Prescription for Your Healing.***

HEALING SCRIPTURES

- Psa. 34:10— *"The young lions do lack, and suffer hunger: but they that seek the LORD shall not want any good [thing]."*
- Psa. 103:3— *"Who forgiveth all thine iniquities; who healeth all thy diseases;"*
- Psa. 119:93— *"I will never forget thy precepts: for with them thou hast quickened me."*
- Psa. 91:3— *"Surely he shall deliver thee from the snare of the fowler, [and] from the noisome pestilence."*

- ℘ Psa. 42:11— *"Why art thou cast down, O my soul? and why art thou disquieted within me? hope thou in God: for I shall yet praise him, [who is] the health of my countenance, and my God."*
- ℘ Psa. 107:20— *"He sent his word, and healed them, and delivered [them] from their destructions."*
- ℘ Psa. 46:1— *"God [is] our refuge and strength, a very present help in trouble."*
- ℘ Psa. 55:22— *"Cast thy burden upon the LORD, and he shall sustain thee: he shall never suffer the righteous to be moved."*
- ℘ Psa. 25:20— *"O keep my soul, and deliver me: let me not be ashamed; for I put my trust in thee."*
- ℘ Psa. 119:107— *"I am afflicted very much: quicken me, O LORD, according unto thy word."*
- ℘ Psa. 121:2-- *"My help [cometh] from the LORD, which made heaven and earth."*
- ℘ Psa. 119:50— *"This [is] my comfort in my affliction: for thy word hath quickened me."*
- ℘ Psa. 116:10— *"I believed, therefore have I spoken: I was greatly afflicted."*
- ℘ Psa. 91:16— *"With long life will I satisfy him, and shew him my salvation."*
- ℘ Psa. 118:17— *"I shall not die, but live, and declare the works of the LORD."*
- ℘ Rom. 8:2— *"For the law of the Spirit of life in Christ Jesus hath made me free from the law of sin and death."*

- Rom. 8:26— *"Likewise the Spirit also helpeth our infirmities: for we know not what we should pray for as we ought: but the Spirit itself maketh intercession for us with groanings which cannot be uttered."*

- Rom. 8:11— *"But if the Spirit of him that raised up Jesus from the dead dwell in you, he that raised up Christ from the dead shall also quicken your mortal bodies by his Spirit that dwelleth in you."*

- Rom. 4:17— *"And being fully persuaded that, what he had promised, he was able also to perform."*

- Isa. 53:4-5— *"Surely he hath borne our griefs, and carried our sorrows: yet we did esteem him stricken, smitten of God, and afflicted. But he [was] wounded for our transgressions, [he was] bruised for our iniquities: the chastisement of our peace [was] upon him; and with his stripes we are healed."*

- Isa. 40:29— *"He giveth power to the faint; and to [them that have] no might he increaseth strength."*

- Isa. 40:31— *"But they that wait upon the LORD shall renew [their] strength; they shall mount up with wings as eagles; they shall run, and not be weary; [and] they shall walk, and not faint."*

- Isa. 50:7— *"For the Lord GOD will help me; therefore shall I not be confounded: therefore have I set my face like a flint, and I know that I shall not be ashamed."*

- Isa. 57:19— *"I create the fruit of the lips; Peace, peace to [him that is] far off, and to [him that is] near, saith the LORD; and I will heal him."*

- Isa. 43:2— *"When thou passest through the waters, I [will be] with thee; and through the rivers, they shall not overflow thee: when thou walkest through the fire, thou shalt not be burned; neither shall the flame kindle upon thee."*

- Isa. 41:10— *"Fear thou not; for I [am] with thee: be not dismayed; for I [am] thy God: I will strengthen thee; yea, I will help thee; yea, I will uphold thee with the right hand of my righteousness."*
- 2 Cor. 2:14— *"Now thanks [be] unto God, which always causeth us to triumph in Christ, and maketh manifest the savour of his knowledge by us in every place."*
- 2 Cor. 10:4-5— *"For the weapons of our warfare [are] not carnal, but mighty through God to the pulling down of strong holds; Casting down imaginations, and every high thing that exalteth itself against the knowledge of God, and bringing into captivity every thought to the obedience of Christ;"*
- 1 Pet. 2:24— *"Who his own self bare our sins in his own body on the tree, that we, being dead to sins, should live unto righteousness: by whose stripes ye were healed."*
- Jer. 30:17— *"For I will restore health unto thee, and I will heal thee of thy wounds, saith the LORD; because they called thee an Outcast, [saying], This [is] Zion, whom no man seeketh after."*
- Jer. 33:16— *"In those days shall Judah be saved, and Jerusalem shall dwell safely: and this [is the name] wherewith she shall be called, The LORD our righteousness."*
- Jer. 17:14— *"Heal me, O LORD, and I shall be healed; save me, and I shall be saved: for thou [art] my praise."*
- Jer. 1:12— *"Then said the LORD unto me, Thou hast well seen: for I will hasten my word to perform it."*
- John 8:36— *"If the Son therefore shall make you free, ye shall be free indeed."*

- John 10:10— *"The thief cometh not, but for to steal, and to kill, and to destroy: I am come that they might have life, and that they might have [it] more abundantly."*

- 1 John 3:8— *"He that committeth sin is of the devil; for the devil sinneth from the beginning. For this purpose the Son of God was manifested, that he might destroy the works of the devil."*

- 1 John 3:21-22— *"Beloved, if our heart condemn us not, [then] have we confidence toward God."*

- 1 John 3:22— *"And whatsoever we ask, we receive of him, because we keep his commandments, and do those things that are pleasing in his sight."*

- Matt. 8:17— *"That it might be fulfilled which was spoken by Esaias the prophet, saying, Himself took our infirmities, and bare [our] sicknesses."*

- Matt. 15:13— *"But he answered and said, Every plant, which my heavenly Father hath not planted, shall be rooted up."*

- Matt. 8:2-3— *"And, behold, there came a leper and worshipped him, saying, Lord, if thou wilt, thou canst make me clean. And Jesus put forth [his] hand, and touched him, saying, I will; be thou clean. And immediately his leprosy was cleansed."*

- Matt. 18:18-19— *"Verily I say unto you, Whatsoever ye shall bind on earth shall be bound in heaven: and whatsoever ye shall loose on earth shall be loosed in heaven. Again I say unto you, That if two of you shall agree on earth as touching anything that they shall ask, it shall be done for them of my Father which is in heaven."*

- Matt. 21:21-22— *"Jesus answered and said unto them, Verily I say unto you, If ye have faith, and doubt not, ye shall not only do this [which is done] to the fig tree, but also if ye shall say unto this mountain, Be thou removed, and be thou cast into the sea; it shall be done. And all things, whatsoever ye shall ask in prayer, believing, ye shall receive."*

- Prov. 3:7-8— *"Be not wise in thine own eyes: fear the LORD, and depart from evil. It shall be health to thy navel, and marrow to thy bones."*

- Prov. 4:20-22— *"My son, attend to my words; incline thine ear unto my sayings. Let them not depart from thine eyes; keep them in the midst of thine heart. For they [are] life unto those that find them, and health to all their flesh."*

- 2 Tim. 1:7— *"For God hath not given us the spirit of fear; but of power, and of love, and of a sound mind."*

- 2 Thess. 3:3— *"But the Lord is faithful, who shall stablish you, and keep [you] from evil."*

- Exo. 15:26— *"And said, If thou wilt diligently hearken to the voice of the LORD thy God, and wilt do that which is right in his sight, and wilt give ear to his commandments, and keep all his statutes, I will put none of these diseases upon thee, which I have brought upon the Egyptians: for I [am] the LORD that healeth thee."*

- Exo. 23:25— *"And ye shall serve the LORD your God, and he shall bless thy bread, and thy water; and I will take sickness away from the midst of thee."*

- Deut. 7:15— *"And the LORD will take away from thee all sickness, and will put none of the evil diseases of Egypt, which thou knowest, upon thee; but will lay them upon all [them] that hate thee."*

- Deut. 7:14— *"Thou shalt be blessed above all people: there shall not be male or female barren among you, or among your cattle."*

- Deut. 28:1— *"And it shall come to pass, if thou shalt hearken diligently unto the voice of the LORD thy God, to observe [and] to do all his commandments which I command thee this day, that the LORD thy God will set thee on high above all nations of the earth..."*

- Deut. 30:19-20— *"I call heaven and earth to record this day against you, [that] I have set before you life and death, blessing and cursing: therefore choose life, that both thou and thy seed may live: That thou mayest love the LORD thy God, [and] that thou mayest obey his voice, and that thou mayest cleave unto him: for he [is] thy life, and the length of thy days: that thou mayest dwell in the land which the LORD sware unto thy fathers, to Abraham, to Isaac, and to Jacob, to give them."*

- Jas. 5:16— *"Confess [your] faults one to another, and pray one for another, that ye may be healed. The effectual fervent prayer of a righteous man availeth much."*

- Jas. 5:14-15— *"Is any sick among you? let him call for the elders of the church; and let them pray over him, anointing him with oil in the name of the Lord: And the prayer of faith shall save the sick, and the Lord shall raise him up; and if he have committed sins, they shall be forgiven him."*

- Heb. 13:8— *"Jesus Christ is the same yesterday, and today, and forever."*

- Heb. 10:23— *"Let us hold fast the profession of [our] faith without wavering; (for he [is] faithful that promised;"*

- Heb. 10:35— *"Cast not away therefore your confidence, which hath great recompence of reward."*

- ꓤ Heb. 11:11— *"Through faith also Sara herself received strength to conceive seed, and was delivered of a child when she was past age, because she judged him faithful who had promised."*

- ꓤ 1 Kings 8:56— *"Blessed [be] the LORD, that hath given rest unto his people Israel, according to all that he promised: there hath not failed one word of all his good promise, which he promised by the hand of Moses his servant."*

- ꓤ Joel 3:10— *"Beat your plowshares into swords, and your pruning hooks into spears: let the weak say, I [am] strong."*

- ꓤ Nahum 1:9— *"What do ye imagine against the LORD? He will make an utter end: affliction shall not rise up the second time."*

- ꓤ Mark 11:23-24— *"For verily I say unto you, That whosoever shall say unto this mountain, Be thou removed, and be thou cast into the sea; and shall not doubt in his heart, but shall believe that those things which he saith shall come to pass; he shall have whatsoever he saith. Therefore I say unto you, What things soever ye desire, when ye pray, believe that ye receive [them], and ye shall have [them]."*

- ꓤ Mark 16:17-18— *"And these signs shall follow them that believe; In my name shall they cast out devils; they shall speak with new tongues; They shall take up serpents; and if they drink any deadly thing, it shall not hurt them; they shall lay hands on the sick, and they shall recover."*

- ꓤ Gal. 3:13-14— *"Christ hath redeemed us from the curse of the law, being made a curse for us: for it is written, Cursed [is] every one that hangeth on a tree: That the blessing of Abraham might come on the Gentiles through Jesus Christ; that we might receive the promise of the Spirit through faith."*

- Eph. 6:10-17— *"Finally, my brethren, be strong in the Lord, and in the power of his might…"*
- Phil. 2:13— *"For it is God which worketh in you both to will and to do of [his] good pleasure."*
- Phil. 4:6-7— *"Be careful for nothing; but in everything by prayer and supplication with thanksgiving let your requests be made known unto God. And the peace of God, which passeth all understanding, shall keep your hearts and minds through Christ Jesus."*
- Rev. 12:11— *"And they overcame him by the blood of the Lamb, and by the word of their testimony; and they loved not their lives unto the death."*

HEALING CONFESSIONS: THE POWER OF THE TONGUE

1. Father, I thank You that above all things I am prospering and I am in good health. Even as my soul shall prosper, my body is blessed; my body is the temple of the Holy Ghost.

2. Father, I thank You that my youth is renewed like the eagles. And, You have forgiven all my diseases! Lord, I curse at the root every sickness, symptom, disease, pain, virus, discomfort and infirmity that has tried to attack my body.

3. Father, I thank You that my body is the Holy Temple of God and God, You are glorified by my total deliverance, healing and divine health.

4. Father, I thank You that I am whole in my body, my organs, in my spirit and every area of my life.

5. Father, I thank You that You have filled me with divine health. My immune system, internal organs, eyes, ears, joints and tissues work and perform perfectly.

6. Father, I thank You that every attack upon my health is destroyed and I'm missing nothing in my health.

7. Father, I thank You that the blood that You shed for me has healed me from every sickness and disease.

8. Father, I thank You for destroying every work that the enemy brings including soul ties to people, addictions, and all activities that would try to cause damage to my physical and mental health.

9. Father, I thank You that You are my healer and that You watch over Your words to perform it. You are living in me now, healing me now, and setting me free now, in Jesus name.

10. Father. I thank You that You bore my sickness so I wouldn't have to. So, satan can't put on me, what Jesus bore for me! Therefore, I am whole.

11. Father, I thank You that I don't have to try to get healed; I've been healing because by Your stripes I am healed.

12. Father, I thank You for destroying the works of the enemy of sickness not just for me, but for my spouse, my children, and my children's children forever; my parents, uncles, aunts and cousins are all healed as well for generations to come, in Jesus' name, Amen.

13. Father, I thank You for Your will being done on earth as it is in Heaven; there is no sickness in heaven; therefore, I am not sick on earth. Jesus is in me and His life flows in me.

14. Father, I thank You for Your promises that all things are possible unto me, and all of the promises of God are yes unto me, for Christ has paid the price for all of them.

15. Father, I thank You that I believe that all things I say shall come to pass; all things which I desire when I pray I believe that I have received them and I have them now, in Jesus name.

16. Father, I thank You that I sow words of health and healing, deliverance, and peace every day and daily I reap health in my physical body.

17. Father, I thank You that I am of God, and have overcome satan. For greater is He that is in me than he that is in the world. I will fear no evil, for You are with me, Your Holy Spirit comforts me.

18. Father, I thank You that no weapon formed against me shall prosper for my righteousness is of the Lord. And whatsoever I do will prosper for I am like a tree planted by the rivers of water.

19. Father, I thank You that no evil will befall me; neither shall any plague come near my dwelling, for the Lord has given His angels charge over me and they keep me in all my ways.

20. Father, I thank You for redeeming me from the curse of the law; therefore, I forbid any sickness or disease to come upon my body; every disease, every germ, and every virus that touches my body dies instantly in the name of Jesus.

21. Father, I thank You that every organ and every tissue of my body functions properly and in the perfection to which God created it to function and I forbid any malfunction in my body, in Jesus' name.

PERSONAL CONFESSION OF FAITH

If you are not born again, please pray this prayer with me, and receive Jesus Christ as your Lord and Savior!

Dear Heavenly Father,

I recognize that I am in need of a salvation because Your word tells me that all have sinned and fallen short of the glory of God (Rom. 3:23). I therefore repent, and turn my life over to You and I thank You for forgiving me of my sins and my rebellion in going my own way in life (Acts 3:19). You said in Your word, that if you confess with your mouth the Lord Jesus and believe in your heart that God has raised Him from the dead, you shall be saved (Rom. 10:9).

I believe in my heart that Jesus Christ is the son of God and I believe that He is Lord. I believe that Jesus went to the cross and paid the price for my sin through His death. I believe that Jesus was raised from the dead so that I could experience newness of life and be right with God. Your word says, *"For with the heart one believes unto righteousness, and with the mouth confession is made unto salvation"* (Rom. 10:10). I do believe with my heart, and I now confess with my mouth that Jesus Christ is now my Lord and Savior; therefore, according to the word of God, I am saved and I am now a child of God! Please, Lord, fill me with Your precious Holy Spirit and empower me to live this new life in Christ Jesus (Acts 1:8). Thank you Lord, and I pray this in Jesus' name, amen. (John 14:13).

WELCOME TO THE BODY OF CHRIST!

Making the choice to become "born again" is without a doubt the most important decision you will ever make in this life. It outweighs career choices, marriage, and financial investments, because it ensures where you will spend eternity – life without end and more glorious than our human minds can begin to comprehend!

Salvation is something that is impossible to earn through our own efforts or good works; instead, it is received as a wonderful and precious free gift. God loved you so much that He sent Jesus to come into the earth, to be born of a woman, and go to the cross and endure a horrible death.

Jesus, being our substitute, has paid the price for our sins. However, because He was sinless, the grave couldn't hold Him and He rose from the dead as the firstborn among many brethren (Rom. 8:29). Your acceptance of this free gift, making Jesus Christ your Lord and Savior, has numbered you among the many brethren, praise God! Yes, a great exchange has taken place. He took all of the unrighteousness that we possessed and gave us the righteousness that He possessed.

The Bible calls this justification and because of your decision, you now stand before God washed and clean as if you've never sinned. Isn't that wonderful?!! You have been brought into a place of righteousness. 2 Cor. 5:21 says, now as a child of God, you have the right to approach God the father through prayer and receive His leading and instructions for life (Heb. 4:16).

As great as the assurance of your eternal destiny may be, salvation also opens doors for victorious living in this life, in the here and now. The word salvation is a powerful word that is meant to bring deliverance, healing, and wholeness to every part of your being, and it affects every endeavor in your life. Yes, the favor of God has been poured out upon you as a child of the king (Psa. 5:12).

I would like to encourage you to begin to nurture this new life through a daily discipline of Scripture reading. It's so important that you build your faith and begin to grow spiritually by feeding your spirit on the word of God. God's word will cause you to become all that He has purposed for you while here on earth. I assure you, that your life will never again be the same! In Jesus' name, amen.

Meet the Author

DR. ERIQ T. HARRIS, SR.

Dr. Eriq T. Harris, Sr. is the senior pastor of Temple of Deliverance Life Changing Ministries in Chicago, Illinois. He is an apostle who oversees and train pastors and also stewards ministry gifts as an author, teacher, and as a basketball coach.

He is married to Lisa F. Harris and together they have 5 children; Brittany, Eriq Jr., Emanuel, Faith and Elijah.

He considers his mission to be one of healing and deliverance through teaching and his vision is to empower ministry gifts in the body of Christ, so that all may grow to their full calling in the Lord.

FACEBOOK: Temple of Deliverance Life Changing Ministries

https://www.facebook.com/TODLCM/?rf=196038543741501